THE FACE
THAT CHANGED
IT ALL

THE FACE THAT CHANGED IT ALL

a memoir

BEVERLY JOHNSON

with Allison Samuels

Foreword by André Leon Talley

ATRIA BOOKS

New York   London   Toronto   Sydney   New Delhi

ATRIA BOOKS
An Imprint of Simon & Schuster, Inc.
1230 Avenue of the Americas
New York, NY 10020

First Atria Books hardcover edition August 2015

ATRIA BOOKS and colophon are trademarks of Simon & Schuster, Inc.

For information about special discounts for bulk purchases, please
contact Simon & Schuster Special Sales at 1-866-506-1949 or
business@simonandschuster.com.

The Simon & Schuster Speakers Bureau can bring authors to your
live event. For more information or to book an event contact the
Simon & Schuster Speakers Bureau at 1-866-248-3049 or
visit our website at www.simonspeakers.com.

Interior design by Kyoko Watanabe

Manufactured in the United States of America

10 9 8 7 6 5 4 3 2 1

Library of Congress Cataloging-in-Publication Data

Johnson, Beverly, 1952–
   The face that changed it all / Beverly Johnson with Allison Samuels ; foreword
by Andre Leon Talley. — First Atria Books hardcover edition.
      pages cm
ISBN 978-1-4767-7441-1 — ISBN 978-1-4767-7444-2 (ebook) 1.
Johnson, Beverly, 1952- 2. African American models—Biography. 3. Models
(Persons)—United States—Biography. 4. Actresses—United States—
Biography. I. Samuels, Allison. II. Title.
   HD6073.M77J63 2015
   746.9'2092—dc23
      [B]
                              2014042346

ISBN 978-1-4767-7441-1
ISBN 978-1-4767-7444-2 (ebook)

Contents

Contents

Foreword

Beverly Johnson made history in 1974. Her story is both powerful and unique.

She was the first African-American woman, a woman of black skin, whose face appeared on the cover of the world's most prestigious fashion magazine, the holy grail of style—American *Vogue*.

Since that defining moment in 1974, Beverly has journeyed on in her life with grace, gravitas, and gold-rimmed guts.

Beverly Johnson shattered the ideological standards of beauty in a commercial domain, introducing a whole new paradigm not only for black women, but for the world and its acceptance of and response to black beauty as a whole. Beverly should be considered among the most important faces to alter the image of fashion, and the entire cultural dynamic, over the last century. Her staggering influence in that world still looms today.

This is the story of an American woman, a role model, and a mentor for so many women, particularly women of color all over the world. And for all of us: I became the first African-American man to break the secret code of the *Vogue* culture when Anna Wintour named me one of the magazine's creative directors in 1983. I flew into that gilded cage nine years after Johnson's historic breakout cover.

Beverly becoming the first black woman to grace the cover of *Vogue* signaled a bold game change in the world of fashion. The year 1974 was a hallmark year because of the courageous decision of Condé Nast and then *Vogue* editor-in-chief Grace Mirabella to use Beverly's image on the front of the revered fashion bible. It was all at once a beautiful and triumphant nod to the 1960s—that eventful and fascinating decade of civil rights, women's liberation, feminism—and a breakdown of the invisible codes of prejudice on the hallowed pages of the gold standard of fashion. And it was only one of the fabulous moments that make Beverly Johnson's life and narrative so wonderfully rich and so fabulously vivid.

Today, Beverly is a strong businesswoman, daughter, mother, grandmother, and a true survivor of life and everything it's thrown at her along the way. She is a true force of nature—determined, fighting back from the brink of destruction—and to this very day she is still just as elegant and just as beautiful as she was on that now-legendary *Vogue* cover in 1974.

If Beverly's life were fiction, it would be a great masterpiece from the very grand Toni Morrison, the Nobel Prize–winning African-American author. If Ms. Johnson's life were a film, it would no doubt be directed by Steve McQueen, whose *12 Years a Slave* won Best Picture at the Academy Awards in 2014.

Beverly is brutally honest throughout and doesn't hold back the tears, even when revisiting some truly heartbreaking life events. She is especially introspective when delving into her seriously troubled second marriage, which ended in an ugly divorce and an even uglier child-custody battle, in which she lost her daughter.

But she fought back and survived it all with grace and style.

In the light of the disco ball, which she aptly calls "smoke and mirrors," where money is big, egos are colossal, and evidence of a noble human spirit is a rare thing, Beverly amazingly managed to survive fame, celebrity, and all the damage it can do to the human soul.

Beverly's journey is one that should inspire every woman from any generation and from any walk of life to keep soldiering on no matter the endless land mines she may come across.

More than just a face, Beverly is a bona fide living legend. As I reached the end of her manuscript, tears of joy welled up in my eyes. Her life thus far is a story that should uplift the human spirit of both men and women. She has lived through it all: adversity, fame, fortune, love, marriage, divorce, marriage again, divorce again, addiction, redemption, renewal of spirit, and just plain life in general. Beverly's history is not just a chronological tale about her rise to the top of the world of fashion, it's also the story of a woman who refused to give up even when the world seemed to turn against her.

Ultimately, Beverly Johnson's story is one of infinite grace and towering strength.

—ANDRÉ LEON TALLEY
CONTRIBUTING EDITOR, *VOGUE*

Ode to Gloria

My mother, Gloria Johnson, always had the most towering presence in my life, all of my life, and what a gift she has been. When I think of my lucrative and history-making career on the covers of so many national and international glossy magazines, I can't help but bring to mind my mother's looming influence.

When my father forbade me from entering the modeling world oh so long ago, it was Gloria Johnson, ever so sweet and proper, who did the unthinkable. She defied my father's wishes and made the phone call to New York to set up appointments for me to be seen by those who could help steer me toward a career that I could have never imagined for myself. My mother rarely defied my father, but that time she did.

Many years passed before my mother told me that she, too, had once dreamed of a career in modeling. But the times didn't allow it, and my mother's prayer remained unanswered. She was determined to make sure my dream didn't suffer the same fate. I think in many ways I fought hard to develop my career in fashion as a tribute to my mother and to make her proud. Deep down inside I knew I was also helping her fulfill the long-lost dream she had been denied so many years ago.

Gloria Johnson was my hero then, and she remains my hero today as she gallantly fights the debilitating effects of Alzheimer's disease. She always said she didn't want to experience pain as she got older, but we never thought she would suffer the pain of a disease that attacks the mind in the way Alzheimer's does. How I loathe this unrelenting disease that has stolen so much of my mom from me and my entire family. Alzheimer's has stolen too much from far too many families, and I pray a cure is close at hand.

The memories that once made my mother laugh, cry, and smile are no longer there. She barely recognizes me or my name now without my prodding, yet she is still the mother I adore, and I'm forever her daughter. The smiles, hugs, and girlish giggles we share together are more precious now than ever. I thank God every day for the gift of my mother and her unwavering support. My mother's love was always deep and always unconditional, and it is that love that continues to sustain me now.

Today, my mother isn't able to remember the story of my rise to the top of the modeling world, nor can she recall her role in helping me get there. But I can assure you she was right by my side every step of the way.

CHAPTER 1

Who's That Girl?

I never really thought I was pretty. Not that I gave my looks much thought at all while growing up in Buffalo, New York.

Let's be clear: There were more than a few attractive people residing in the Johnson family household. We can start with my mother, Gloria, then move on to my two gorgeous sisters, Joanne and Sheilah; but not me. Never me.

So how exactly I ended up being the one with a coveted invitation to spend an evening at the home of designer Roy Halston Frowick for one of his legendary gatherings on this particular day was a true mystery. Though my sisters Joanne and Sheilah were the girls every guy in our neighborhood drooled over at first sight during my childhood, I was the Johnson girl who later moved to New York to model for major magazines. No one saw that coming, least of all me.

It was August 1973, the height of Halston's glory days on Madison Avenue, and there I was standing on West Sixty-Third Street, trying my best to figure out where exactly I was going. It was the hottest summer afternoon I could remember in New York City, and the heat wasn't doing my perfectly layered makeup any favors. I hurried down the street, in heels of course, trying to read the house numbers. It seemed like the sun's powerful rays were the universe's way of punishing me for jumping out of the cab before I had my bearings.

Even though I was still in my early twenties, my life had already become an endless blur of appointments, interviews, and meetings. My likeness had already begun to appear on a bevy of magazine covers and in advertisements, but I was just learning how to navigate the peaks and valleys of what that exposure really meant for me.

Since this wasn't quite the adult life I had envisioned for myself while growing up, I was still adjusting to the madness of running from one photo shoot or fashion fitting to another. The sheer weight of the logistics could easily frazzle anyone's nerves on any given day. If that weren't enough, I was also encountering some self-inflicted personal drama in the form of an ex-husband who refused to comprehend the true meaning of "ex."

Many days I found myself just trying to keep my head above water. Don't get me wrong, I loved the life I was living, but I wasn't always prepared for the nonstop demands and pressures it presented. Somehow I had gotten on a fast-moving roller-coaster ride, and I wasn't at the controls.

Still, even with all that background noise in my head, I couldn't afford to be out of sorts that afternoon. I had to appear flawless when I entered Halston's party, and flawless is what I was determined to be. There could be no clothing mishaps, and no evidence that my perfectly applied makeup had encountered that sweltering New York City day.

While I was enjoying a booming career in the world of high fashion at that time, I knew I had really arrived when I received an invite to a dinner party at the home of one of the world's most prominent designers.

Halston was by far the most celebrated and influential designer of the seventies, and I loved him something fierce. Everyone did. Halston—one name was all he needed—emerged as the first billion-dollar fashion designer in the world of haute couture and single-handedly developed the blueprint for the likes of Oscar, Ralph, Calvin, and Diane to become household names the world over. Until Halston appeared on the scene, most of the highly respected, famed, and grand design houses were located in Europe, in either Paris or Milan. Halston would change that the day he created a pillbox hat for Jacqueline Kennedy to wear as she watched her husband take the oath of office of the President of the United States in 1961. After that major coup, Halston's designs routinely graced the bodies of some of the world's most stylishly stunning women. Fabulous ladies such as Lauren Hutton, Princess Grace of Monaco, Ali MacGraw, Bianca Jagger, Liza Minnelli, and Lauren Bacall were photographed regularly in his couture designs.

Then of course there was me. I'd always been fascinated by each and every aspect of the fashion industry, and Halston was the first to take my call when I yearned to learn even more. He agreed to put me in his runway show at a time when well-known print models, which I was at the time, rarely did such a thing. Runway modeling was considered a few steps beneath print during the sixties and early seventies. But that did little to discourage me from wanting to be on the runway. As far as I was concerned, a rule wasn't a rule until somebody had the gall to break it.

Thankfully, Halston was happy to oblige me. Early one week in 1973, I strolled along in his show wearing several of his slinky halter-neck dresses and wide-legged jersey trousers. I loved every minute of it! Despite my initial terror of sashaying around a room filled with potential buyers and New York socialites, my first foray into the world of runway modeling had been as seamless as one of Halston's pricey cashmere designs. Simply put, I nailed it! After the show on a Tuesday, Halston casually mentioned a little dinner party at his home that Friday and suggested I stop by.

Stop by? Of course I would stop by! Yes, I had a modeling assignment for *Glamour* magazine on the island of Saint Martin the day following the show, Wednesday, and wouldn't be returning until Friday afternoon. But a little thing like being out of the country wasn't going to prevent me from accepting one of the most desired invitations in town. Halston was the king of the New York social scene, and his parties were as legendary for their ambience and fine dining as they were for their cachet and megastar power.

Halston personified everything that made the crazy seventies the decade many people wish they had been part of. It was a sparkling new age that seemed to belong exclusively to the young, or at the very least the young at heart. The baby boomers of today were actually teenagers back then, which means those years were all about exploration and experimentation. Sex, drugs, and rock and roll ruled the day, every day. But it was also a decade in which people searched for their identity and for truth, including me. Halston embodied all of that complicated seventies angst in his talent, in his style, and in the manic way in which he lived his public and private life. And I wanted to be in the middle of it all.

But first I had to get to his party. The actual logistics were complicated. The dinner began at 7:00 p.m., and my plane didn't land back in New York at JFK until 4:00 p.m. If you've ever tried to get from JFK airport to Manhattan at that time of day, you know what a nightmare it can be. There was a fifty-fifty chance I'd make it on time, but nothing was going to stop me from trying. I was in luck—my cabdriver seemed to think he was driving in the Indy 500, and though I kept thinking that I really would rather not succumb to the flames of a fiery car accident just to get to a party—not even Halston's—we somehow made it to my apartment safely and in good time.

Which was good, because the party was sure to make the top of Liz Smith's celebrity gossip column in the New York *Daily News* the next day. After debating half an hour what to wear to my first big-city party, I chose a long black jersey cape over a matching long black dress. But it wasn't a Halston, even though I had a closet half-filled with his designs. (Note to self: You really should wear the design of the designer to his dinner party.)

Those days were long before the era of personal makeup artists arriving at your house before an event. That night I had to do my own, and I think I did a pretty jam-up job, if I do say so myself. My hair was pulled back in its usual neat bun and my silhouette was chic, slim, and sleek. Once I was ready, I grabbed yet another cab and raced from my West Forty-Eighth Street apartment to the Upper West Side soiree. Fortunately, I found that my "face" had stood up well against the smoldering August heat, as I finally found the famed 101 West Sixty-Third Street address. I arrived looking exactly like the version of Beverly Johnson most expected to see out and about in the big city.

I entered the designer's glass-façade town house and stopped dead in my tracks; I couldn't believe I was still in New York City. Halston had transformed what had originally been an eighteenth-century carriage house into a virtual oasis, a more-than-seven-thousand-square-foot home solely created for him to peacefully exist in his own space and time, completely oblivious to the concrete jungle just outside his door.

I steadied myself as I stood in the huge foyer and tried my best to take in everything that was going on. In front of me, a staircase seemingly floated in the air, like a mini catwalk, and on it the seminude bodies of models Pat Cleveland and Sterling St. Jacques danced to Sister Sledge's "He's the Greatest Dancer." As I watched them, Halston appeared and glided down the rail-less staircase. The designer's suave movie star looks nicely complemented his tanned skin, model-like height (six feet, two inches), and freshly styled salon hair. He was wearing his signature uniform: black cashmere turtleneck sweater, formfitting suede jacket, dark trousers. His left hand held his ever-present long cigarette while his right hand waved at the crowd of friends gathered in his living room.

Halston loved nothing more than throwing parties for his famous friends, stars like Andy Warhol, Candice Bergen, Anjelica Huston, and Margaux Hemingway. I watched my dear friend as he was surrounded by people who hung on his every word. Who could blame them? Halston had an incredibly endearing way of telling a story that made every detail come alive and dance before your very eyes. And boy did that man have stories to tell about the unbelievable life he had lived, from growing up in Iowa to his years in New York.

And when he wasn't throwing his own parties, he could be found holding court at the infamous Studio 54, his home away from home. Halston wasn't just the toast of the town—he was the toast of the entire fashion universe, and he wasn't shy about tooting his own horn to let you know about it, either. Halston actually wasn't shy about anything!

Eventually the crowd parted and I got a quick hug and a kiss from the man of the hour, and then he was gone again. I decided to take a further look around his unique and elegant home. Fireplaces roared in eighty-degree temperatures, there were bamboo gardens in the backyard—complete with mirrors to reflect light back into the house—and as if that were not enough, the house boasted a rooftop deck the size of a baseball field! It was breathtaking!

The legendary architect Paul Randolph had been responsible for the interior design, which was awash in various tones of white and gray. Those colors mixed perfectly with the furniture, upholstered as it was in the same knit flannel Halston often used in his clothing collection. Gray was a color Halston thought looked good on just about everyone and everything, so even the floors in his home were covered in a gorgeous gray velvet carpet. Adding to the sense of restraint, my dear friend Halston avoided using a lot of artwork on the walls, and there wasn't much in the way of accent pieces, either. It was haute, and minimalist, and all quite spartan.

After I completed my tour, I noticed that Pat and Sterling, who had previously been dancing seductively on the catwalk, were now mingling with the crowd. Sterling, an absolutely beautiful black man, had a small (well, not so small) cup covering his private parts, while Pat was now gleefully free of any clothing at all and proudly showcasing everything for all to see. She was particularly interested in highlighting the fact that her pubic hair had been waxed into a perfectly defined heart shape. I was completely taken aback (one of the many times that night) when I heard her ask people their opinion of her new design.

Pat's exhibitionist ways turned what I had hoped would be a fabulous night of fun into something rather uncomfortable for me. She was the only other black woman in attendance and now she had become the "show" for the evening. I suspect that Pat had done her homework and discovered that the easiest entrée into that world was simply becoming the night's exotic entertainment. By "that world" I mean the white, upper-crust, very wealthy one that few blacks ever got the chance to witness, much less enter. Performing for the crowd was Pat's hall pass through the front door, I suppose. It seemed to have unlocked many doors for her, but I guess my twenty-one-year-old mind just didn't fully understand or appreciate Pat's thought process that night.

In the wake of the civil rights movement, I felt obligated to those who had fought and died for my right to be treated equally. There were so many who had marched and sacrificed their lives so that I could have a place in the mainstream world of fashion and even attend that party that night. Maybe Pat felt the same but just had a very odd way of showing it.

Juggling the knowledge of this country's volatile racial past while navigating the hippie movement of the seventies would often put me at great odds not only with others in the industry, but with myself at times, too. Whereas the sixties demanded a certain amount of social responsibility, the seventies demanded the complete opposite.

Halston's designs and Pat's unabashed nature defined an era known for both its luxury and excess, and they were two vices that became far too comfortable for far too many of us.

There were other vices, too. Cocaine was Halston's drug of choice, and all of his dinners offered a large supply of it. The drug was presented in small salad bowls alongside tall glasses of champagne. As my relationship with Halston grew, I regularly observed him enjoying his daily intake of the three c's; caviar, champagne, and cocaine. We sometimes joked with each other that water simply had too many calories! It all seemed so fun and harmless back then.

With Pat's heart finally out of view, I made my way through the throng of guests to the dining room. In the middle of the room there was a rather odd-looking Lucite block table that easily could have been confused with a large slab of Antarctic ice upon which Elsa Peretti–designed votive candles and Tiffany flatware had been placed. There was also a marble-topped cocktail table, numerous hassocks, and some people were even eating on the stairs. Halston's best-buddy-for-life Liza Minnelli always ate on the stairs, and that night there she was, in her favorite spot, laughing it up as she drank glass after glass of champagne.

Waiters were beginning to serve the meal created by Halston's charming live-in assistant, Mohammed Soumaya, so I decided against joining Liza on the steps and instead cozied up to the Lucite table for a sampling of the meal du jour. And what a meal we dined on that night! Crudités for starters, followed by an entrée of blanquette de veau, and Halston's favorite, a baked potato topped with caviar. (Later, I would learn that though the entrée menu varied from party to party, that side dish rarely, if ever, changed.)

As I began to eat, I briefly looked up and found myself staring at the most beautiful pair of violet-hued eyes I'd ever seen in my life. In fact, I'm quite sure I hadn't seen a pair of violet-colored irises ever until that night. Sitting across from me was the grand dame of all grand dames, Ms. Elizabeth Taylor, in all her legendary glory.

I knew she and Halston were great pals and that he'd designed a number of her most beautiful gowns, but I'd never imagined for a moment that I would be in the same room with her. But there she was, looking exactly how I'd have imagined she would, and more. She was incandescently beautiful, with the most gorgeous porcelain skin and a head full of glossy dark-brown hair. I had to force myself not to stare. She said, "Hi," but all I could manage in return was, "I love your ring."

That night she was wearing the famed Taylor-Burton diamond, given to her by her then estranged husband Richard Burton. I had followed every detail of their torrid love affair in the popular Hollywood gossip magazines, including the story of that ring. From what I'd read, Liz clearly lived her life unconcerned with how others felt about the decisions she made. I had tremendous respect for her for just that reason. I think she also lived by the motto that life was too short not to look amazing every day, so she never left home without dripping in millions of dollars' worth of bling. I had a tremendous amount of respect for that, too!

Yes, Liz had other gems, stones, and diamonds, but none like the diamond she wore that night. The original rough diamond had been found in 1966 in the Premier Mine in South Africa and cut into a pear shape by jeweler Harry Winston. Burton had engaged in a fierce bidding war with shipping magnate Aristotle Onassis just to get his hands on that diamond, and he eventually purchased the 69.42-carat ring from Cartier for $1.1 million in 1969, making it the most expensive diamond in the world at the time. Now that's real love for you.

As I gazed at that storied piece of jewelry, Liz Taylor said, "You like it, you wear it."

Without missing a beat, she pulled the ring off her finger and threw it across the table. I caught it in midair and slipped it on my finger just to see how it would feel to wear something so rich with history and love.

I won't lie. For a moment I fantasized that I was the owner of that amazing rock, waving it around for all to see as I explained that my newest BFF, Liz Taylor, had recently gifted it to me on a whim.

My fantasy didn't last long. As I much as I loved the ring, I had an even stronger desire to get it back to Ms. Taylor as quickly as possible. Lord knows the last thing I needed in my life was to lose, or even run the risk of losing, Elizabeth Taylor's history-making, million-dollar ring. I could just see Liz Smith having the time of her life in her column the next morning were such a mishap to take place. But before I could hand it back, Ms. Taylor wandered off to chat with other people, though I'm quite sure she could see me out of the corner of her eye. Clearly the woman known for playing roles in films such as *Who's Afraid of Virginia Woolf?* and *Cleopatra* was having a good old time watching me sweat. I figured her throwing her huge diamond ring to some poor unsuspecting soul was one of her favorite party tricks, done just for laughs.

After what seemed like forever, Liz came back to our large block of ice and motioned for me to come sit next to her, giving me the chance to finally return her ring. With all the stories about her historic Hollywood career and rocky personal life, I honestly didn't know what to expect as I made my way to sit by her side. What in the world would I talk about with this woman I'd watched all my life on the big screen? Or should I breathe a word at all?

Thank goodness she was nothing like what I expected. She told me that Halston explained to her a while ago that I was the new and beautiful "It Girl" and now she wanted to know more about me.

I may have been the It Girl of the moment, but she was the It Woman of all time as far as I was concerned! Why would she want to know more about me?

As the dinner party began to wrap up and the beautiful people in attendance began making their pilgrimage to their next stop on the party train, with Halston leading the way, I decided to head in the opposite direction. I wasn't in the mood for Studio 54, which was no doubt where they were all headed. I needed to go home and prepare for my next day of work.

I wasn't much of a club girl. I needed to get some rest so I'd be ready for my next close-up! I wouldn't get it hanging from the rafters at Studio 54. So I took my third cab of the day and headed home.

CHAPTER 2

Smile

In the taxi on the ride home from Halston's dinner party, my mind was spinning!

Home was now my new—but still very empty—apartment in Midtown Manhattan, the one I had shared with Billy, my still somewhat-present and ever-clingy ex-husband. I hopped out of the cab to find the same overdressed pimps hovering outside my building; inside, oversized rodents ran around in what was supposed to be my one-bedroom haven.

It's safe to say my real-estate choices in the big city left much to be desired. It was also safe to say I wouldn't be inviting my new BFF, Liz Taylor, over for drinks anytime soon.

How had I gotten to this magical (if sometimes contradictory and confusing) place from where I'd started?

Nothing in my life up to this point could have prepared me for the world I found myself in. To be honest, I don't think anything could have prepared me—not even my mother's wisest words of wisdom. Which was odd because there was a time when I thought Gloria Johnson had an answer for everything.

For as long as I could remember, my mother had always offered each of her children the most deceptively simple yet amazingly effective advice. And it worked! One day, for example, I was changing into my after-school clothes in the bedroom of our modest two-story home. As I did most days, I was telling my mother all about my school day. For good measure, I decided to share with her my fear that I didn't have enough friends. At the time, my next-door neighbor Dada Bratton was my one and only friend in the whole entire world. Although I loved Dada dearly, I felt I needed to expand my personal circle somehow.

My mother's advice? If you want more friends, smile more.

As luck would have it, not having a multitude of friends as a child was not the first clue my mother had that I'd likely be the most offbeat of her five children.

I was born smack-dab in the middle of two girls and two boys, and without question I was the only bona fide introvert in the gregarious Johnson clan. I certainly wasn't the one in the family who turned all the heads. My sister Joanne was a year younger than me, and a shade or two lighter in complexion, which during those years made a world of difference. She was petite and short, too, with curves in all the right places. I often wished I looked more like Joanne. She was also very charming, and that won her friends, too, particularly boys.

My older sister, Sheilah, was pretty easy on the eyes as well. But her beauty was something all together different from Joanne's. In her bare feet, Sheilah stood nearly six feet tall, and her skin tone was a beautiful golden brown, just like our father's. But it wasn't Sheilah's height or her blemish-free skin that made her a big standout. Whereas Joanne's brick house of a body caused quite a stir wherever she went, Sheilah's trademark was her thick, silky head of hair that grew like a weed in summer; it thoroughly refused to comply when she finally decided she wanted to get down with Black Power and grow an Afro. (By the way, my sisters are still knockout beauties to this day.)

I was born right between them and had neither long silky hair nor light-colored skin. I was simply an African-American nerd. Brown, lanky, and painfully shy, I always had my head in a book. I read nonstop, between classes and late at night, everything and anything, from James Baldwin to Pearl S. Buck. My books meant the world to me, because they allowed me to escape to faraway places and helped me avoid unwanted eye contact with people.

So while my siblings enjoyed an endless supply of friends during our childhood, I had more serious things on my mind. Keeping my grades up was one of them, and resisting the girls who bullied me anytime the opportunity presented itself was the other. These were little roughneck girls who waited for me at the school bus stop, ready and willing to start a fight for no reason. Apparently Regina, Betty Ann, and Rita from down the street thought that my being taller than most of my classmates and making straight As in all my classes were good enough reasons to give me constant grief.

So with only a few friends of my own, and with the threat of a regular beat down hanging over me, I turned to swimming. When I wasn't reading, I was swimming or teaching someone else how to swim. I loved the water, and I usually swam before school in the morning and for a few hours after school was done. My father once lovingly teased me by saying that I was as dark as a copper penny due to the fact that I stayed outside in the sun all day during the long summer months. He didn't say it as an insult, but that was the era of "light being right," so my feelings could have been hurt. But I hadn't planned on using my looks (such as they were) for much of anything as I got older anyway, so I thought nothing of it. Instead, I was planning on a future in law. It was the end of the 1960s, and I'd been profoundly influenced by my heroes, Dr. Martin Luther King Jr., Malcolm X, and President John F. Kennedy. I wanted to somehow continue their work, and the best way I could see of doing that was by becoming a lawyer.

But along with my dreams of being a lawyer, I spent most of my preteen and teen years pursuing my dream of becoming a world-class swimmer. Being under water allowed me to escape from those mean girls at my school. Spending time at the pool every day gave me the chance to sidestep, as much as humanly possible, that awkward and unenviable Odd Girl Out title that every kid, no matter who she is, dreads with a passion.

Too bad I wasn't able to live under water 24-7.

But what about my mother's advice to smile more often? Well, I decided to try that simple exercise one day in Mrs. Miller's science class. Mrs. Miller was my favorite teacher, and when she asked me to read the class assignment out loud, I did so with a huge smile plastered on my face. I also threw in a joke here and there. Thankfully, I drew a few giggles and smiles from classmates who up to that point had completely ignored me. Mission accomplished—or so I thought.

After class, I received a couple of high fives, as well as a note from Mrs. Miller to give to my parents. Mrs. Miller liked me, so I didn't give the note much thought.

Big mistake. When my mother read the note out loud to me later that night, I discovered that it suggested I had been boisterous in class and that my jokes were out of place and uncalled for. I was close to tears, but my mother was just plain angry. Not at me, just to be clear. My mother's first and only inclination was to come to my defense, given my consistent record of excellent grades and exemplary behavior. She didn't understand why Mrs. Miller hadn't just pulled me aside to ask why I had done something so out of character. Maybe something was wrong with me that day or I just needed some extra attention for some reason.

Gloria Johnson was something else, especially the way in which she fought to protect her children whenever she felt they were under attack.

My mother's calm and pleasant demeanor hid a fierce dedication to her home and family. That's not to say that my mother was the type to offer long, mushy hugs at bedtime, or kisses whenever you made the honor roll or won class queen for the year. She was a traditional, old-school southern African-American mother, one who worked hard to make sure all her children were well fed, clothed, and protected from the elements. That was true motherly love as far as she was concerned. She wanted nothing but the best for her children and she made sure each of us had it, but overt acts of affection and outward expressions of emotion weren't a part of that package.

I came to realize that this behavior was pretty typical of my mother's generation down south. I can't imagine that tenderness was something she was shown a great deal of as a child, given that she was born when her own mother was just thirteen years old. My grandmother, "Mother Dear," as we called her, was forced into an arranged marriage to a much older man. My mother was the result of that marriage, and I think it's pretty fair to say that love had nothing to do with it. The arrangement didn't last very long—one version says my great-grandfather got wind of physical abuse toward my grandmother and my grandfather went missing under "mysterious" circumstances.

I assume that since my grandmother was still a young child herself it was decided that raising my mother was just too much for her. So my mom was sent away to boarding school up north. Little black girls attending boarding school was a rarity during the thirties and forties, but my mother wasn't big on sharing the details, so I never got the chance to hear much about those days. Black folks from the South, particularly those who struggled through the challenges of postwar America, often kept their personal lives private. No amount of prying could or would get them to open up about what they'd been through, and it was an unspoken rule to respect their wishes.

Though I never learned the details, boarding school is where I believe my mother developed her impeccable sense of style and grace, attributes that she still carries with her to this day. My mother was always refined and elegant. It would be a few years before I developed that type of elegance or grace in my own life, though. After my classroom reading fiasco, I reverted back to my old ways of keeping to myself, hanging out with my neighborhood friend Dada, and devouring my favorite books to pass the time. I continued to devote myself to swimming every morning and afternoon, which saved me from more confrontations with the mean girls from my neighborhood. But that didn't last very long, either.

Right before I entered junior high school, the girls and their beef with me hit fever pitch. One day, an entire group of them met me at the bus stop on my way home and beat me up. Dada, my one and only friend in the whole wide world, was there by my side and went down swinging with me. We got our butts kicked real good that day.

The entire neighborhood was buzzing for days about the incident. My parents were pretty angry, but what could they do about other people's kids? What could anybody do? My ego might have been hurt a little, but I played it cool, as was my way, and made a plan to get revenge as soon as I could.

It was important for me to make certain those girls and their hateful pranks didn't haunt me throughout my junior and high school years. I had to find a way to put a stop to it. I wouldn't live with that kind of fear, so with Dada along for the ride, we figured out where every girl would be over the following few days. Then we worked out how we would approach them individually to return the ass-whupping in kind.

We didn't have to go find Betty Ann. She literally walked past my house one afternoon while my family and I were all sitting outside on the front porch talking and enjoying the day. It was my lucky day! I bolted inside the house to get myself ready for a good old-fashioned girl fight!

Fighting black girl–style takes some preparation. For me at least, it meant earrings off to avoid torn earlobes (very unattractive, not to mention painful) and a significant amount of Vaseline evenly applied all over my face to prevent unsightly dark marks and scars.

Though I had absolutely no idea then that I would become a model one day, I always protected the face.

Vaseline applied, I hurried back downstairs, passed by my parents and siblings, and yelled, "I'll be right back."

Halfway down the block, I screamed out Betty Ann's name, but she kept on walking—in fact, she actually had the nerve to pick up her speed after glancing back and seeing me closing in on her. All of her sassy boldness was nowhere to be found that day. With my long legs it didn't take me long to catch up to her. When I did, I landed the first blow to the top of her head and she hit the ground with a loud thud. And that was it—it was all over! No blocking or ducking required. Though I'd wasted a good dollop of Vaseline, it was worth it. I never had a problem with Betty Ann, or any of those girls, again.

If only I could have slain *all* my childhood demons so easily.

Like any young girl wanting to earn some spending money, I would often babysit for families on my street. One family I worked for, the Browns, were pretty good friends with my parents, particularly Mrs. Brown. I was quite comfortable in the Browns' home, so things usually ran smoothly when I babysat there. I did my homework while the kids played, and I made sure they were sound asleep by the time their parents returned from a night on the town.

Most evenings, when I heard the Browns' car drive up, I readied my things for Mrs. Brown to drive me home. Mr. Brown would usually come inside first to ask if all was well and to pay me. But one particular evening, Mr. Brown, a short and stocky man, walked through the front door and with a strange look on his face headed directly toward me. I was dressed in a white turtleneck, jeans, and boots, and I had my coat in one hand. Before I knew what was happening, he reached out and grabbed me, knocked me to the floor, and began to grope my breasts. I was twelve years old. I was horrified. Wasn't this man a friend of my family's? How could he do this to me?

Dazed and upset, I fought back and managed to get Mr. Brown off me with one big shove. I ran out of the house as quickly as I could and into the car with Mrs. Brown. I was out of breath, with my hair scattered all over my head. Mrs. Brown asked me if I was OK. All I could say was a quiet "Yes," as I tried hard to fight back tears while she drove me home.

When I think back, I really believe Mrs. Brown knew what had happened to me inside her home that night. Sometimes women look the other way when their husbands do unspeakable things to other women. Sometimes they look the other way because they feel helpless to do anything about it. Sometimes they are just grateful it isn't happening to them.

Molestation wasn't a topic discussed with your parents, friends, or anyone else in those days. There wasn't anyone I felt comfortable enough with to talk to about the nightmare that had just happened to me. I didn't know what self-esteem was at twelve years old, but what Mr. Brown did that night ripped away whatever I had of it. I had to find my own way of coping with an incident that I didn't even fully understand.

A few days later at another babysitting gig, I filled an empty baby bottle with some Scotch from the family's home bar and quietly sipped on it all night. I hadn't done that before, but I needed something to help me forget what had happened and drinking seemed to do the trick for everyone else—why not me? I even took the bottle to school the next day and took sips whenever I thought no one was looking. Why drowning my sorrows with alcohol made sense to me at just twelve years old, I'm not completely sure. But I'd watched my father enjoy his own libations long enough that I figured anything that lifted his mood could surely do the same for me. For a short period that day at school, I felt like I was on top of the world, but by lunchtime, I'd thrown up all over my desk and felt like my head was floating away from my body. The school called my mother and she came to pick me up early. I silently thanked God that she didn't ask why or how I had gotten so sick. A part of me will always believe she knew the answer already. We drove home in total silence.

(Years later, after I had gained some fame as a model, I would have the opportunity to confront Mr. Brown. I was home one day when he and his wife came over to visit my parents. They congratulated me on my success and made small talk. I looked Mr. Brown in the face and asked, "Molested any young girls lately?" If a black man's face could turn red, his would have that night. He was shocked and ashamed, and both he and his wife rushed out of our house without saying good-bye. That felt pretty good, I must say.)

But that feeling of vindication was years away. At just twelve years old, being molested by a neighbor was one more reason to avoid the prying eyes all around me. There was one exception to that rule however. Though I kept my distance from most other people out in the world, due in part to the bullying and the abuse, I always longed for the attention of one person in particular—my father.

I yearned for more time with my dad, quite possibly because he worked such long and grueling hours at the local steel mill for most of his life. My father was one proud former military man. He stood six feet, three inches tall, and was blessed with glistening bronze skin, strong chiseled cheekbones, and a powerful sense of self-worth that stayed with him to his dying day. My father always paid his dues, and nothing stopped him from providing for his family.

I really can't say for sure if my father's stringent work ethic was directly connected to his own parents. My paternal grandparents made for quite the awkward pair. My grandfather was a small Native American who stood only about five-foot-three. My father got his considerable height from his mother, an African-American woman who was, like my father, almost six-foot-three. I remember thinking at her funeral that her coffin was the longest one I'd ever seen.

My dad was raised up north in New Jersey and was in many ways the polar opposite of my mother, who hailed from the Deep South. Gloria, despite her proper pedigree, saw the world for what it really was—cold, hard, and oftentimes mercilessly unfair to those with darker skin tones. My father, more often than not and much to his own detriment, saw the world through rose-colored glasses. He thought life could be fair and just. Sadly, he had his heart broken many times because of that overly optimistic point of view. I'll always believe the reality of racism wore him down and caused him to begin drinking more heavily over the years. My parents' conflicting views about life would dramatically influence each of us children in vastly different ways as we all grew into adulthood.

Rarely would we kids ever have the chance to discuss with our parents the horrors of slavery, the injustices of Jim Crow, the evolving work of Dr. Martin Luther King Jr., or the work of the NAACP. We were living in the middle of the civil rights movement, yet my parents simply went about life as if those historic events—like integration, or the bravery of Rosa Parks—were occurring in an alternate reality.

On a few occasions I even heard my father chastise Dr. King for bringing more trouble black people's way. In my father's convoluted way of thinking, Dr. King was just stirring an already boiling pot. He couldn't see the larger picture or the positive changes that would eventually come for people of color as a result of Dr. King's stance on racial equality. My father was brilliant, and full of love, but he also had flaws.

Despite those flaws, my father was still my hero, and if you ever caught him at 5:00 a.m. on any given school morning during my childhood, you'd know why. I still vividly remember my father lovingly preparing our school lunches while at the same time methodically checking all of our homework assignments. I treasured every moment of our predawn chats. We would talk about life; I would tell him about my previous day at school, my progress on the school swim team—anything, in fact, to keep him focused solely on me. For thirty minutes every morning, everything in my life was fine.

CHAPTER 3

Girl on Fire

Things got much better for me once I entered high school.

I became the first black cheerleader at my high school, even though it hadn't been a real goal of mine. Alas, it didn't last long in any case, thanks to my darling baby sister, Joanne.

During one game night, little Miss Joanne got into a brawl with some other girls. Joanne was as cute as a button and could get any guy she wanted anytime she wanted, but she couldn't fight worth a damn. Being the big sister, I couldn't just let her get beaten up right in the middle of my spelling out letters. So I left my cheerleading post and ran up into the stands to help her so she wouldn't get pummeled.

The day after the fight, I was thrown off the squad for leaving my post and fighting. They had never wanted a black girl on the squad in the first place so they gladly welcomed any opportunity to get rid of me, whatever the reason. My dear mother, bless her heart, promptly challenged the decision, but it didn't change a thing. I was off the squad after just three games.

I tried not to let my short-lived cheerleading career get me down, or, for that matter, my uninspiring love life. My romances, such as they were, were with my sister Joanne's rejects. She would tell me that she'd broken up with some guy, and then give me his number to call. And like a true fool, I would! That's how badly I wanted somebody, anybody, to like me.

But besides boys, my main concern was getting accepted into a good college after high school. The importance of higher education was something my parents talked about all the time. I think most black people in my parents' generation thought the same thing. Education was the be-all and end-all, the great equalizer for people of color.

Even though Tim and Gloria refused to discuss the civil rights movement with us, I made sure to follow it at every turn. One day I'll never forget is April 4, 1968, when Dr. King was assassinated in Memphis, Tennessee. My entire high school was in an uproar. After everyone gathered in the gym, I was given the microphone as the only black member of the student council so that I could speak to the student body. Usually, when I appeared on stage it was to a chorus of boos—that day, I pleaded with my fellow students to remain calm and respectful in the wake of this horrible tragedy. Instead of boos this time around, the kids paid attention to me, and there were no further disruptions or outbursts until the buses arrived to take the students home early that day, though there were riots on the streets of Buffalo in the days that followed.

Then there was the day Robert Kennedy visited Buffalo after announcing his run for president in 1968. His motorcade drove right past our high school, and we all ran behind the red convertible as he waved and shook hands. Call it fate or just sheer luck, but I was one of the few students he reached out to, and he shook my hand. I realized I had just touched the hand of someone ready, willing, and able to take his late brother's place in history, so it broke my heart that Robert Kennedy's life was cut short before he ever got that chance.

The summer of 1969 was my last at home before leaving for Northeastern University in Boston. My mother got me a summer job in a ritzy women's store. Who knows why Gloria Johnson thought her second-oldest daughter should work in a clothing store. I wasn't a clotheshorse of any kind, and we couldn't afford the clothes sold there even if I had been.

The Jenny Shop was located in the center of town and featured expensive, high-end designer apparel that only the most well-paid and elite people could afford. That was not my family. Adding to my unhappiness was the fact that they rotated the song "Raindrops Keep Fallin' on My Head" (the theme from the popular 1969 Paul Newman and Robert Redford movie *Butch Cassidy and the Sundance Kid*) nonstop throughout the day. I heard that song so many times that summer I thought I'd have a nervous breakdown if I heard it again. But though I really would have preferred to be working my old job teaching swimming at the YMCA, Gloria Johnson knew what she was doing. The job she secured for me selling fine women's "rags" would change the course of my life in a matter of months. I was the only black salesclerk in the upscale boutique, a fact that spurred me on to work harder than everyone else. In almost no time, I became the top-selling clerk. I gained that title despite being shady whenever Dada and her family came in to shop. When I say they shopped, I actually mean they came in and purchased the least expensive items they could find in the store. That's really just browsing. That's where I came into the mix.

For instance, Dada would buy a five-dollar headband or a ten-dollar handkerchief. Then I would go into action and throw in a few extra trinkets of much more value free of charge! Now, my guess is the manager was aware of the five-finger discount I was providing my friends and family. But since Dada and her family were pretty much the only blacks who ever walked into the store for months at a time, she figured it wasn't worth the fuss to mention it. And I figured since I was forced to hear that damn song all day long, it was a fair exchange.

The manager of the Jenny Shop was a French woman called Mimi. Because her accent was so strong I could barely work out what she was saying, so I would just nod my head. But there was one thing she said to me regularly that I understood clearly:

"You should think about becoming a model."

No one had said that to me in all my seventeen years, and the thought had certainly never crossed my mind. Fashion was never discussed in the Johnson home. *Ebony* was the only magazine found on our coffee table, and we read it for the news articles on black history, not the fashion. Mimi's suggestion was meaningless in my world at that time, so I didn't mention it to my mother, my sisters, or Dada. I was going to become a lawyer, and that was that.

Mimi kept at it, though. On my last day at work before leaving for college, she hurriedly jotted down the name of a woman in New York who could help me get started in modeling if I were ever to change my mind. I just smiled and tucked the piece of paper in my wallet and headed off to college in Boston, where a brand-new world of higher learning, girlfriends, boyfriends, and life experiences was awaiting my arrival.

~

Northeastern wasn't exactly my first choice for where to spend the next four years, but it was the school that gave me the most scholarship money, and that was the real determining factor. Also, I enrolled sight unseen, because with several college educations to pay for, my parents just didn't have the financial resources for travel to check out different campuses with their children. It was a shock to arrive and find out just how huge the place was.

The beauty of the campus, with its wide, rolling lawns, wasn't matched by what I found inside. My white roommate clearly hadn't imagined she would be sharing living quarters with someone of a much darker hue, and she wasn't very pleased. She didn't utter one word to me the entire first year. That wasn't all—she would see me reading my history book and turn off the light anyway!

That was my life during my freshman year, and it was pure hell. Tim and Gloria Johnson had to hear about it via very expensive collect phone calls from the hallway of my dorm every week. My father got such an earful one week that he yelled through the phone, "Beverly, just come on home! You hate it that much there, just come home."

But I couldn't just give up and run back to Mommy and Daddy like some big baby loser. Fortunately, a bunch of older and much wiser female students (a mixed group of both black and white) overheard my tearful exchanges with my parents on the phone and were kind enough to take me under their wing. They taught me how to navigate the massive campus more efficiently and also brought me along to all the best parties, at Northeastern and on nearby Harvard's campus, too. Things were finally beginning to look up for me. I loved my new girlfriends with a passion. I had no idea this was only the appetizer!

CHAPTER 4

New York, New York

As my first year of college came to a close, I was looking forward to my summer job as a swimming instructor at the YWCA in Roxbury, Boston. That is, until I heard the news that it had been axed due to city funding cuts.

Now what was I going to do, without employment and with little time to find a new job? Go back to Buffalo? Not on your life! Leave it to my "girls" back at the dorm to think of something. Sitting in our room one day, cramming for end-of-the-year exams, one of my girlfriends, Beverly Gamble, casually said, "Why don't you try modeling?"

The familiar sound of those words sent a chill down my spine, but this time, given the fact that I desperately needed a job, I wasn't so quick to dismiss the idea.

"Will somebody please explain what this modeling deal is all about?" I said.

My friends pulled out a fashion magazine and pointed to a picture of a tall, skinny white girl wearing a gorgeous dress. Well, if that's all there was to modeling—holding a pose, wearing fabulous clothes, and taking pictures all day—I could do that easily. And I still had that little piece of paper in my wallet from Mimi at the clothing store, the one with the New York contact on it. Let the modeling begin!

But nothing is ever that simple.

At the time, I was totally unaware that there were prominent black models, such as Helen Williams, Donyale Luna, and Naomi Sims. All were beautiful models with vastly different profiles, and all had risen to a certain level of success in the fashion world during a wave of political correctness in the mid-sixties. The background stories of their work and struggles in the industry were rarely, if ever, told, so I had no idea who they were or that they even existed in the first place. These women were not showcased prominently in *Ebony* magazine because the magazine didn't cover high fashion at that time. Maybe, just maybe, if I had known a bit more about those women's stories in the modeling game beforehand, I would have been able to navigate my own course through the world of fashion a little smarter. Too late now.

~

But then there was also the issue of my parents to navigate.

Tim and Gloria Johnson would need to OK my plan of moving to New York that summer to model high fashion. In hindsight, I realize that the phone call home that day to share my newly minted idea was one of the funniest conversations I ever had with my parents. Modeling, in my father's mind, was pretty much on par with being a streetwalker. Where Tim Johnson got some of his ideas I do not know.

"So you're going to New York to be a prostitute?" my father yelled through the phone the day I announced my new plans.

My heart sank.

While my father ranted, my mother stayed cool and just calmly listened as I explained how the idea came about.

None of this convinced my father. He continued to say no, and 99 percent of the time, when my father said no, that ended the conversation. But something had piqued my mother's interest. I'm not sure if it was the idea of modeling per se, my modeling, or her daughter having the opportunity to explore uncharted territory. Whatever her motivation, she never explained, as was her way. She just allowed my father to believe the subject was closed and then maneuvered behind his back by calling the woman Mimi had suggested and arranging for us to meet her in New York the following week.

I was really blown away by my mother's efforts to help me enter a world that neither of us knew a thing about. She obviously thought modeling could make my life a lot better, and she was right, but I'm not sure she ever understood the ripple effect she began in my life with that single phone call. I was so accustomed to seeing her as a one-dimensional person that I never stood still long enough to see the many layers and contradictions hidden beneath the surface. I guess I was too young to understand that there was more than met the eye when it came to my mother's personality. It was a lesson I would learn the hard way many, many times, and about a lot of people.

A week later, on a June day in 1971, my mother and I rode Amtrak to New York City and took a room at a small hotel near Times Square. Our appointment the next day was to meet Korby Pleasant, Mimi's friend, who also managed what we came to know was a legendary store, Jax's Fifth Avenue, a small boutique that sold one-of-a-kind designs and exotic imported fabrics. (My mother and I had never heard of the store.)

Rumor had it that Korby knew just about everyone in the industry. She was of mixed heritage, but she could pass for white at first glance, and she appeared to be in her mid- to late forties. She was probably one of the most effortlessly chic women in all of New York

City, and her entire presentation from head to toe had to be impeccable every day if she wanted to stay at the helm of one of the hippest stores along the entire eastern coast. Jax's usual class of customers was a fascinating mix of New York's society, such as C. Z. Guest and Leona Helmsley, as well as internationally recognized style icons like Lena Horne and Jackie Kennedy.

Jax's kept them coming, in part because it was the first luxury store to introduce one-of-a-kind fashion items such as women's pants featuring a very stylish side zipper. I know that doesn't sound exciting today, but in the sixties it was a very big deal. Jax's also famously sold luxurious Egyptian cotton T-shirts in various pastel hues for a mere $125 each—again, this was in the 1960s. Jackie Kennedy favored this particular trend and was often photographed wearing one while out in the streets of New York.

The day I met Korby, I decided to keep my look clean and simple. I put my slightly curly black hair up in a topknot and kept my face free of heavy makeup. For years, my daily look usually involved a dab of rouge for my cheeks, a hint of black eyeliner, and a bit of cherry-colored gloss for my lips, nothing more. I rarely wore foundation in those days because I really didn't need it, and finding the right color as a brown girl wasn't the easiest thing to do. Companies such as MAC and Fashion Fair didn't exist at this point, so there weren't many options for a girl like me. I put the health of my skin down to my mother force-feeding me a daily dose of cod liver oil during my entire childhood. I hated the taste of that stuff going down, but I believe to this day that's why I have such clear, wrinkle-free skin.

As for my outfit, I chose a white jumper that was actually shorts, which matched perfectly with a pair of flattering black flats to complement my five-foot-nine-inch height. Not exactly the everyday New York uniform, but quite eye-catching.

I had never stepped into a boutique like Jax's before in my life. There was nothing close to this back home. On the inside, Jax's featured gorgeous mahogany walls, but there were no shelves. Instead, designer apparel was brought to the client from the rear of the store. I was intimidated, but my mother and I found Korby to be just as fabulous and gracious as we had hoped she would be. Her genuinely warm greeting immediately soothed my rattled nerves, and I was grateful for that.

For a few minutes the three of us chatted, and Korby asked why I wanted to be a model. Eventually, a few customers arrived, and she excused herself to attend to them. As we waited for Korby to become free, the most beautiful man I could imagine waltzed into the store. He looked like the prince out of a Disney fairy tale, and I was spellbound.

Harry Belafonte. The most successful Caribbean-American pop star in history, the man dubbed the "King of Calypso" for popularizing the Caribbean musical style with the international audience in the 1950s, a man who was a popular movie star as well as a respected civil rights activist. And to Korby, he was a man who could help her decide on my model-worthiness. That's right—the woman who knew everyone also knew Harry Belafonte, and she asked him if I should become a model.

Harry nodded his head as he looked me up and down. You would have thought he was in the middle of a car showroom, selecting the best-looking style and color for that year. He said very few words to me while all this was going on. As for me, I was in a daze. All I could think was, How did the beautiful Harry Belafonte become so perfect and, more to the point, how had he just become a part of my team?

Eventually, Belafonte's wife arrived at the store looking for her husband. She just stood there with a blank stare on her face, which was really more than my eighteen-year-old mind could process. I knew nothing of their domestic situation, and all I was trying to do was to get into modeling. I couldn't tell if Harry's wife was standing there like that because she routinely checked up on ol' Harry or because she was particularly worried that Korby was introducing us. Whatever the issue, it wasn't my problem.

I just needed Harry's seal of approval to kick my career off right. And that day, I got it.

~

Thanks to my mother's excellent ironing technique, my outfit was wrinkle-free for my big meeting at *Glamour* magazine the next morning.

I had chosen to pair a white flared skirt with a matching white blouse this time, along with white knee-high socks and black-and-white saddle Oxford shoes. I carried a pair of white gloves and kept my hair in the same sleek topknot I had worn the day before.

The Condé Nast offices at that time were located in the landmark Graybar Building next to Grand Central Terminal in Manhattan. After being escorted into the waiting room, we watched editors, writers, and designers running around, trying to put together one of the many magazines that were published under Condé Nast's large umbrella. Through the years the company has owned *Vogue, Vanity Fair, Glamour, House & Garden, W, Allure,* and *Self* magazines.

While we sat waiting, and as I grew more nervous about what was to come, someone asked if I would mind taking a typing test. Now I was really confused, not to mention angry. Why in the world, when I had come there to be a model, would I need to take a typing test? I was told that I needed something to fall back on just in case modeling didn't pan out, and my dear mother saw nothing at all wrong with this and urged me to take the test. But I had my own backup plan, thank you very much. It was called a college degree. And why was it any stranger's job to worry about my "fallback" plan? I hadn't fallen *into* anything yet! Still, to please my mother, I took the test. I remember exactly what I typed: "The brown cow." And that was the end of that! No one asked me about typing again that day.

If I needed something that badly to fall back on, I would go to work at the local Dairy Queen.

Finally, I was brought in to meet Alexander Liberman. He was the art and editorial director for all of Condé Nast's publications—translation: He was one powerful man.

Liberman wore a well-fitted navy blue suit, crisp light-blue shirt, and paisley-print ascot, which nicely highlighted his strong English accent and impeccable manners. He showed me around the gigantic room where he had been studying some stunning photographs of gorgeous models smiling up from brightly lit boxes. As we walked, he asked me a few rudimentary questions about myself, then abruptly bid me farewell. I had been there no more than ten minutes and had no indication of his thoughts about me at all. Had I passed or failed?

I didn't have to wait long for an answer. Mr. Liberman's assistant contacted me the same day and told me to head to a *Vogue* photo shoot at Bert Stern's studio.

At the shoot I was placed with a group of models already famous for posing for *Vogue* magazine. There was Veronica Hamel, Karen Graham, and Lauren Hutton, three legends in the modeling game. (There would be little evidence on that day of the pivotal role Lauren Hutton would play in my life much later on. She would prove to be an invaluable aid in my fledgling career. But that was to come.)

After that initial shoot I was told I had been chosen to join a ten-day photo shoot with *Glamour* magazine that would be held on Fire Island in two weeks. I was—officially—on cloud nine!

My mom and I returned to Buffalo buzzing with the news that I had landed my first assignment to model professionally. I couldn't wait to share the news with the entire neighborhood, which really meant my only friend in the whole wide world, Dada. My father was less than pleased and chose to ignore the topic altogether. Though thrilled with my good news, my older brother, Leon, asked if I had told the magazine publishers in New York about my better-looking brothers and sisters.

I tried to relax over the next few weeks, since there really wasn't much preparation for me, as an eighteen-year-old, rail-thin teenager, to do for the photo shoot. Still, that didn't stop my brain from wondering if I should be doing more. Somehow, the thought popped into my head that it couldn't hurt to lose a few more pounds before I stood before the cameras again. Dada's mother, who always carried a little extra weight due in part to her excellent cooking skills, floated the idea that I could take laxatives to get slimmer. That wouldn't be the last time I would hear about extreme remedies for weight loss. The thought of going to the bathroom nonstop didn't seem like the way I wanted to spend my summer. I figured it would be safer if I stuck to riding my bike around the block a few times a day.

July finally came around, and I headed to Fire Island for my *Glamour* magazine shoot.

I hadn't traveled to Fire Island before, even though it was the largest island on the outer barrier parallel to Long Island, New York. Fire Island attracts a large gay population year-round. I wasn't aware of that fact in 1971, but I was given a quick introduction to that world the moment I stepped off the ferry from the mainland.

A group of men, who I assumed were gay, were waiting at the dock and began dancing. Naturally I felt the need to join in, and we danced to the beat of the pounding drums through the streets all the way to the rented house.

If only the entire ten days of that shoot could have been as jovial as that festive dance on the dock. *Glamour* magazine had hired a well-known European photographer to photograph the fashion spread, but he was no friend of mine from the start. I was there to do a ten-page spread by myself, which was a huge deal for me. This was my first real modeling job, so I wanted to be on the set early every morning to prove I was up for the challenge. The photo shoot was to take place outside the house the magazine had rented for us all to live in. By all of us, I mean the photographer, his assistants, the magazine's editors, and me. With the hope of helping things along, I rose extra early to apply my standard makeup plus a little extra since I would be in front of the camera. My rah-rah attitude didn't help, unfortunately. The photographer criticized my look the moment he saw me and instructed me to go back to my room and scrub my face, not once but twice, to remove every speck of the makeup I'd applied. He then mocked every pose I tried to strike, and yelled at me to just stand still as he snapped shot after shot. I'm glad I didn't break or bend easily, even at eighteen years old.

What was with this guy?

I had no idea what I was doing—this was, to repeat, my first solitary modeling gig—and I was sure someone from the magazine had told him as much. But I was learning as fast as I could and I was trying as hard as I could. He seemed like such a jackass, but I had no idea just how much of a jackass he would turn out to be.

Late that first night, as we were all heading to bed, the photographer tapped me on the shoulder and asked me to come to his room to talk about that day's work. Again, being eighteen years old and very naive, I welcomed the chance to set things straight. Silly me. I walked to his room ready to apologize for all my missteps and to ask for a fresh start. Well, that old jackass had something else on his mind. He was lying in bed with his shirt off and a smirk on his face. For half a second I was confused. Why did he invite me upstairs if he was already in bed? He motioned for me to come sit next to him and his big fat stomach. *Ugh!*

Then, I realized talking was not to be on the menu that night. My photographer clearly wasn't interested in discussing the day's work, so I got out of there as quickly as I could. I sprinted back to my room and locked the door behind me. But he followed me, and tapped on my door lightly, so as to not wake up the others in the house, I guess. My head and heart were pounding as his knocks on my door grew louder by the minute. Surely everyone else in the house heard something! But no one said or did a thing. That's the business for you.

What was I going to do? I couldn't call my parents, because that would have been the end of my modeling career. Eventually he gave up, and I finally fell asleep in my bed, quietly praying that he wouldn't return.

As I was falling asleep, it struck me that this photographer had underestimated me. He didn't know that I was the black girl who'd been bullied and booed all the way through elementary and high school. I was the black girl whose roommate had refused to acknowledge her presence for most of her freshman year at college. But he soon would find out that I was the black girl who certainly was not about to be run out of her first big-time fashion shoot by some rude, horny, fat, hairy, white photographer. Not Beverly Johnson.

The next day at the photo shoot, he acted as if nothing had happened. Good choice, since that's exactly the way I acted as well. Even better, he treated me with the respect I had deserved in the first place. First major shoot done.

～

My sophomore year of college began without a hitch, and a few of the magazine layouts with my editorial spreads featured in them began to hit the newsstands. The *Vogue* issue came out, then *Glamour*, as well as an *Essence* fashion layout I'd done that summer. I was particularly proud of that one. Students I'd barely ever spoken to began to recognize me. Even my racist roommate from the previous year had the nerve to open her mouth long enough to say hello. I couldn't believe it and almost ignored her, but then figured I would be the bigger person.

Part of my curriculum at Northeastern University was their co-op program, which stipulated that I had to work one semester and study the next. I was supposed to spend my winter semester that year employed by companies that were connected to my majors, law and political science. But this now posed a major problem, as the modeling assignments were starting to trickle in and turning them down felt foolish, given how well they paid. I really needed the cash if I wanted to keep going to school. My sister Joanne was about to enter Fordham University, and the financial strain on my parents having three kids in college was beginning to take its toll. I wanted to help them out in any way I could.

None of this mattered to my school. They must have heard this kind of sob story from other students a thousand times, but that didn't stop me from making the case that modeling was the perfect job for my major. I gathered all my recent magazine layouts and presented them to the dean of political science, explaining to him that offers for modeling jobs were coming in and that they would be a fine substitute for my legal and political science work. The dean pointed out that the law and modeling were polar opposites, but eventually he agreed to let me use my modeling gigs to fulfill my work credits. Everything was falling into place exactly the way I had hoped.

CHAPTER 5

The Goal

Who doesn't dream of making it in New York at some point in their life? If I can make it there, I'd make it anywhere, right? I took a calculated risk heading to the Big Apple during the winter of 1971–72, but it was one I ultimately felt I couldn't let pass. At barely nineteen years old, what did I have to lose? I couldn't tell if there was a future in modeling awaiting me, but there was a still, small, and very deep voice that seemed to keep whispering, This is your destiny.

That same voice also kept whispering in my ear about the possibility of a future with a superfine guy I'd met on the basketball court the previous summer. I had been introduced to Billy Potter by my good friend Beverly Gamble, and our first date had been akin to something out of a romantic novel. We went to the movies to see *Love Story*, starring former model Ali MacGraw and Ryan O'Neal. From there, Billy wined and dined me big-city style, after which he wooed me with a long kiss I thought would never end as we made our way to his friend's penthouse apartment. On the ride up in the elevator, I felt like I was floating on air.

Once we were alone, I learned that Billy had a tried-and-true system. There were candles, great music, and the ever-present blunt. All this led to a great night of laughs and lovemaking, Billy Potter style: I can still remember having to fight to see his gorgeous face through the haze of marijuana smoke that magical evening.

~

They didn't make guys like Billy Potter back in Buffalo. Billy was an authentic New Yorker. I think that was what stirred my attraction to him when I saw him on the basketball court the summer before. He had a swagger and a quiet confidence, and I got to know that he was suave, extremely clever, and worldly. But best of all, he wanted me in that world. This was the love I'd always wanted, the love I'd been looking for when I took my sister's leftovers in high school.

But I was still very young, and it would take a while for me to fully understand that all love isn't necessarily good love. Even today, I struggle with the notion that there is both good and bad love. As far back as I can remember, I have passionately believed that love of any kind can be the most wonderful gift any human being can experience. Even if that love ultimately comes with a harsh or painful lesson once it's over, the gift of love is always the reward. In the end, aren't we the sum total of all the people we have loved in our lifetime? Even though I've loved and lost many times in my life, I still remain loyal to the same basic philosophy that all love teaches us, or all love leaves us with something valuable in the end. I have to believe that, or what's the point?

Relocating to New York for the winter was not just about Billy, or love, or even modeling. The move also reunited me with my younger sister, Joanne, who was now a college student in the city. We roomed with my mother's aunt, Madeline, but sadly she was sinking deeper and deeper into dementia. Her illness made it clear that I would have to find somewhere else to lay my head sooner rather than later. Joanne was attending Fordham University and could return to the dorms there anytime. I was the one in dire need of a place to stay. Billy, the man I was crazy about, would soon become my man with a solid plan.

In the meantime, Korby offered me a part-time job as a sales clerk at Jax's Fifth Avenue. It was the perfect gig to put extra spending change in my pocket as I got my modeling career under way. She made it clear that I was free to head off to any "go-see" (a modeling audition) or photo shoot, as long as I gave the store management enough notice. As heavenly as the job appeared—and it *was* heavenly, given that I could sneak out and wear Jax's amazing clothes to the go-sees—the money I made still wasn't enough to pay the rent on a New York City apartment. Even in the early seventies, prices for apartment rentals were ridiculous. Rents ranged anywhere from $400 to $700 a month for a one-bedroom in the high-end neighborhoods in which I felt I belonged.

The other heavenly part of the job at Jax's was the opportunity to connect with a pretty large group of famous people who came in to shop. The most mesmerizing shopper for me was Jackie Kennedy. Whenever I served her, she would sweetly smile and say, "Hi, Beverly," in her wispy, girlish voice.

Around this time, the talk of the town was that her second marriage, to Greek shipping magnate Aristotle Socrates Onassis, was in serious trouble and that the two were now separated. It was said that this was the reason she had recently moved back to New York from Greece. I could only imagine the strain she must have felt from such an intense breakup. Though we weren't friends, Jackie was a personal hero of mine—as she was for many women in America. And she *was* a friend, at least in my head, so it really pained me to watch her struggle with yet another heartbreak.

On one particular visit to the store, Jackie rushed in in tears, her Secret Service detail following a few steps behind. She was looking for Korby, who had become her trusted friend and confidante. As if on cue, the entire staff exited the back room, where Korby had been working, so as to give the two women their privacy. This happened two or three times while I was employed at Jax's. To be a fly on the wall of the back room that day would have been something else, but we all respected Korby and the former first lady too much to eavesdrop.

Most of Jackie's shopping sprees to Jax's were brief, but you could tell a lot from what she bought. One sunny morning she rushed into the store wearing the rumpled clothes I presumed she had worn the night before. She had a lunch date at noon and didn't have time to return to her lavish Fifth Avenue apartment to change. So Jackie stopped by Jax's to scoop up a new outfit for lunch, then hurried off with a quick wave and a smile from beneath her signature oversized black sunglasses.

On a side note, for many years I would often see Caroline Kennedy and John Kennedy Jr. at a pay phone near an old apartment of mine at Eighty-Ninth and Madison Avenue. This was the eighties, pre–cell phones, so I imagine the then teenagers were making calls to friends away from mom Jackie's prying ears. When John got older, I would often see him out at the clubs in New York and marvel at what a gorgeous young man he had turned out to be. In a way, I was relieved Jackie was already gone when his plane crashed that July weekend in 1999, killing him, his wife, and his sister-in-law. Losing her son, losing either of her children, would have been too much of a loss for Jackie to bear.

~

Meanwhile, Billy and I were really clicking.

Prior to Billy, I'd only slept with one other guy. I'd met Victor through my older sister, Sheilah. He had attended college with her at the University of Buffalo. But Billy and Victor were complete opposites. Billy wasn't that much older than Victor—just a couple of years—but those years made all the difference. Billy had mastered the art of how to treat a lady exactly the way she wanted to be treated. He took particular pride in his craft, and completely understood what true romance was all about, and how the mind and body had to be joined together to cement any real intimate connection. In other words, he really got it. He got all of me, too, which in turn made for a very happy me, for a while at least.

What complicated matters early on for us was the fact that Billy didn't have his own place. He did, however, have friends in New York who would lend him their apartments whenever he wanted quality alone time with me. It wasn't the perfect arrangement, but Billy would really go all out to make everything just right. Along with the candles, he always made sure that John Coltrane, Duke Ellington, Nina Simone, and Thelonious Monk were in heavy rotation all night long. He knew those larger-than-life jazz greats had been unfamiliar to my ears before we met. My parents weren't big jazz fans and preferred the soulful sounds of Sam Cooke and Jackie Wilson. But now, because of Billy, I had a new love for jazz.

Billy Potter turned my world upside down with his disarming wit and sly charm. But his intellectual gifts often distracted me from some unpleasant realities. Billy had attended some college here and there over the years, but he had never developed a trade he could use to support himself, or anyone else for that matter. Despite that, Billy was the first man I ever encountered who routinely wore custom-made suits, pants, and shirts. My own father, a man who held a real job his entire life, shopped off-the-rack because he couldn't afford such luxuries. Billy, who balked at the notion of full-time employment, wore specialty clothes year-round.

Billy also had a passion for smoking marijuana on a fairly regular basis, which in itself wasn't a big deal for that era (just as it isn't now). Unfortunately, I would soon learn that Billy enjoyed selling weed, too. That fact maybe explains why Billy had so many friends ready, willing, and able to loan him their apartments. His drug connections opened the door for many free things, such as the custom-made clothing. Did all this make me flinch a bit? Yes, it did—a little—though, in hindsight, not nearly enough.

Spotty employment was the primary reason Billy lived with his parents in their modest-sized brownstone in Brooklyn. William and Richardean Potter were two of the most adorable people I had ever met, and that only added to my blurred vision when it came to their eldest son. I mean how could you not love a woman named Richardean? His mother wore that name with all the style it required, and I loved her like she was my second mother. Their younger son, Jimmy, was even more dashing and debonair than Billy, and I really bonded with him, too. Jimmy had the most easygoing and loving spirit of anyone I ever met. But the big city got to Jimmy, and he fell victim to a deadly drug addiction as a young man. He would pass away from his struggle with drugs before he turned forty. But William and Richardean Potter were good, upstanding, hardworking folk trying to make an honest living in a world and a city where it can be pretty tough to do so.

Mr. Potter worked as a paramedic while Richardean worked for the telephone company as an operator. Ever dedicated to both of her children, Richardean regularly tried to get Billy to work at the phone company. Billy would go along with it for short periods, but the key word is "short." Working as a phone company repairman was far too boring for someone with Billy's high-minded ideas about himself. I also suspect Billy began offering customers "products" that had little to do with Ma Bell.

My suspicions were confirmed whenever we met for lunch at the café near the phone company's office. Every time we had lunch, a lot of the employees seemed to know Billy by name, regularly walking up to the table to say hello. The phone company in New York City had to employ hundreds of people, so how exactly could so many of them know one lowly repairman?

Still, even with all that going on, I continued to turn a blind eye to Billy's behavior, as my love for him kept growing. I was sure he felt the same, and I was happy that the deep affection I felt for his parents seemed mutual. When Billy told them about my aunt's failing health and my housing woes, they suggested that I move into their two-and-a-half-bedroom apartment with them.

I still laugh today about that arrangement. My parents would not have agreed to let a boyfriend of mine move into our home for any reason at all. It wouldn't have mattered how dire his circumstances were or how much I loved him. But Billy's parents were the best support system for a girl like me, because they were so accepting and loving.

As for Billy himself, he really did love me, but he had periods where he really resented me, too. That resentment manifested itself in various ways, mostly through acerbic and condescending remarks toward me in which he suggested I was no match for him intellectually and so I would be wise to sit silently when certain topics were discussed. Sometimes he even criticized my intelligence in front of people. That was the toughest part for me, because it seemed as though he was trying to embarrass me. I just didn't understand why.

So many times I wanted to call his bluff and say out loud, "If you're so clever and smart, why are you allowing your woman to pay for everything and do everything? Why are you allowing your woman to take care of you?" But I never did.

Today's men increasingly don't give a second thought to allowing women to take care of them financially, but back then it was something men found embarrassing. I never challenged Billy about how he let me pay the bills. I tried to ignore his slights and insults, chalking them up to his own insecurities. Billy wasn't a vicious man, nor was he mean-spirited, so I chose to let his attacks on me pass.

Still, life only allows us so many opportunities to bury our heads in the sand. One circumstance came my way during our relationship that would demand my attention completely. There would be no avoiding reality, no looking the other way this time.

After dating Billy for less than six months, I discovered that I was several months pregnant. How in the world did I allow this to happen? As my siblings and I had reached high school, my mother sat each one of us down, because she was all about equal opportunity, and regularly reminded both her sons and her daughters that she had already raised five children. She wanted us all to keep that in mind in case we should ever consider bringing a baby home before we got married or were still in school. What she was trying to make sure we understood was that her baby-raising days were over.

Now here I was nineteen years old, unmarried, on the verge of a new career, and with a child on the way. What was I thinking? Clearly, I wasn't doing much thinking at all. I was so in love with Billy, and we were young, free, and living in the moment. Who doesn't want to live like that, right? But living in the moment has consequences, and I had to face mine.

Even though I hadn't shared the news yet with my family, some of my nearest and dearest were smart enough to figure it out. My younger sister, Joanne, was the observant one in the family—nothing slipped by her. She blew my cover when I flew home to Buffalo in the summer of 1971 to attend my older sister Sheilah's wedding. We were all in the back of the church changing into our bridesmaid's dresses when she loudly commented on my additional weight gain.

"Are you pregnant?" she said to me point-blank.

I wanted to smack her in the head for asking me that question in the church, and so I did.

Honest to goodness, we started fighting right there in God's house! Rolling around on the floor of the church in our terra-cotta–colored bridesmaid dresses until Gloria Johnson yelled for us to stop because the wedding was about to start. We suddenly came to our senses and began to fix each other up, patting each other's hair down and straightening our dresses.

Surely my mother and sister Sheilah both noticed the weight gain in my face and body as well, but both simply chose to stay silent. Lord knows, Gloria Johnson was the master of avoiding un-happy topics at any cost. Discuss the unplanned pregnancy of her unmarried daughter? Not on your life!

There was no discussion of any kind about my pregnancy once I returned to New York City. Billy knew someone willing to do the abortion, even though I was further along than was recommended. Of course he did—Billy knew people willing to do just about any-thing. Looking back, I realize that I was simply too young to under-stand what was really about to happen to me. Even though I could have died, I was too immature to worry about all the things that could go wrong medically. Had I told my mother or my older sister what I was about to do, things would have been different. They would have warned me about the dangers of doing that procedure at that stage of the pregnancy, and would have probably talked me out of going through with it. And that's why I didn't tell them.

The day I chose to end my pregnancy, I knew I would have to become emotionally numb if I wanted to make it through, so I turned myself into a kind of zombie. I felt every bit of the physical pain from the procedure, but nothing more. Emotionally, I had to block out the idea of aborting my unborn child if I wanted to keep my sanity, and I didn't want to start second-guessing myself. My heartbreaking decision to terminate my pregnancy was the right decision for me at the time, and I had to trust that. My future, and everything about my world, was much too uncertain at that point to bring another life into the confusion. Billy stood by me every step of the way, and I was thankful for that.

Though I had some discomfort, and was a bit bloated, I went right back to work in the days afterward to keep my mind from wandering. I had to try not to think too much about what could have been. Love was grand and all that, but I had goals that I wanted to reach, and I couldn't allow them to be derailed by anything or anyone. Not even my own poor choices or bad timing.

I remember exactly the point when I decided I wanted a long

career in the modeling industry. I had to take steps early on to avoid the now-you're-here-and-now-you're-not outcome. Shortly after the Fire Island trip, I began to ask the makeup artists, cameramen—and anyone else on my early shoots for *Glamour*, *Vogue*, and *Essence*—a host of questions about what my next move should be if I wanted to stick around as a top model.

A lot of the answers were the same: my next best move would be to get an agent. And not just any agent—I should reach out to the biggest agents out there if I wanted to truly make it in the long run. I did my research and I found there was no one bigger, bolder, or better than Eileen Ford.

Eileen Ford started the Ford Modeling Agency with her husband, Gerard, in the mid-1940s, and by the 1960s she was at the helm of one of the top modeling agencies in the world. For a model, Ford had in her mind the ideal height, the proper spacing of the eyes, and the correct proportions of cheekbones, breasts, and hips, and in doing so she set the standards for models for much of the latter part of the twentieth century. In a business sense, Ford revolutionized the beauty industry and created the template for the modern, multimillion-dollar modeling agency. In 1971, she was indeed a uniquely powerful woman to behold.

And while I wasn't the usual girl on the roster—she tended to pick blondes with blue eyes as her ideal—I can testify that she certainly changed the life of this nineteen-year-old black girl.

CHAPTER 6

Friends and Foes

"Too fat."

Those were the first two words ever uttered to me by the legendary Eileen Ford. I was attending an open call for models at her deluxe offices, which were located in Midtown Manhattan and featured two supersized red double doors as you entered. The waiting room where all young women were escorted resembled the huge floor of the New York Stock Exchange, with the same amount of frantic activity. Agents on their phones sat behind desks booking jobs for supermodels like Lauren Hutton, Christie Brinkley, and Cheryl Tiegs, among others. At the center of it all stood their fearless leader, Eileen Ford, a small, rather nondescript lady with the exception of the massive crop of brown frizzy curls on the top of her head. She often referenced that mass of hair as "nappy." She would often say her hair was similar to black people's hair.

I had been so hopeful when I walked in, but with a swift wave of her hand she shooed me away like a bothersome fly.

Up until that point I was fairly certain my path to modeling nirvana led directly through Eileen Ford and her agency. But Eileen's hasty assessment of my body fat ratio suddenly put those plans on hold.

However, my intuition had told me to make sure I didn't put all my eggs in one basket, so I'd already been visiting other agencies in case Eileen Ford didn't want me on her roster. For those visits, I had a set uniform I loved to wear: a long tweed coat, which all the major stores were featuring in their front showroom windows as the hot item for fall, matched with a pair of sky-high platforms that easily rivaled the pair Herman Munster wore each week on *The Munsters*. Why I thought I needed to wear a tweed coat in midsummer, or to put on a pair of five-inch heels to pound the concrete streets of Manhattan, is something I'll never be able to explain. The day after I wore those shoes, I would have blisters on my feet so huge, so painful, I could barely move from my bed to the floor.

But even though I was considering additional options in my search for an agent, Eileen Ford was still my first choice. While she had dismissed me with those two cruel words, I'd already been through enough in my life that I didn't break down in tears or run out of the room. In retrospect, I realize I could have mentioned the photo shoots I had already done for *Vogue*, *Glamour*, and *Essence* to someone at the agency that day. In truth there wasn't really time, and I had just assumed the modeling agencies would see in me the same traits the editors of those magazines had seen, whether they knew I had already modeled before or not. I was wrong.

Had the magazine shoots I'd just completed all been flukes? Had I just been in the right place at the right time? Had Harry Belafonte been off his game that day when he gave his stamp of approval at Jax's?

I'm blessed that self-doubt didn't have much time to take root in my mind.

Just three days later, an assistant from Eileen Ford's office called Beverly Gamble's parents' home, where I was staying, and asked if

I could go back for a meeting with Mrs. Ford. I arrived bright and early the next morning at the Ford Agency to find the same room that had been filled with bodies and earsplitting noise now empty and absolutely still.

Eileen Ford suddenly appeared and with a completely straight face said to me, "Beverly, you have lost weight!"

All I could do that day was offer this fierce, powerful woman my best and brightest smile in response to the very best of her bullshit. I had been in her offices just three days before and since that time had enjoyed a few Good Humor strawberry shortcake ice cream bars. I hadn't lost a single damn pound—in fact, I may have even gained a few. But that was my first, free-of-charge introduction to the world of smoke and mirrors.

With that one statement, though I didn't know it at the time, Ford was painting me a crystal-clear picture of an industry that I would find to be overflowing with a toxic mix of deceit, manipulation, abuse, and backstabbing. It's clear now that she wanted me to appreciate up front that any success I enjoyed in the game of modeling would surely be followed by a certain level of betrayal, heartbreak, and disappointment, caused not just by enemies but also by those nearest and dearest.

Eileen Ford had had a significant hand in crafting the success stories of an endless array of notable beauties that spanned several generations. As well as Lauren Hutton, Christie Brinkley, and Cheryl Tiegs, she'd handled Martha Stewart (Martha modeled in her early years before becoming a homemaking goddess), Candice Bergen, Jerry Hall, and Ali MacGraw. Now she was on board to do the same for me.

In the midst of enhancing my professional portfolio courtesy of Eileen, I also enrolled in courses at a local community college. It didn't seem that I would have the chance to return to Northeastern University anytime soon, and I still wanted a backup plan just in case. Around this time I began receiving heftier paychecks from my modeling work, thus allowing me the opportunity to give back to my parents and to save for the future. Much as it did on my father's, financial security weighed heavily on my mind, so I put away every dollar I could. Lavish shopping sprees were not a part of my routine.

If the work Eileen got me and night school weren't enough for me to deal with, I also decided to walk down the aisle with Billy Potter. We were basically inseparable by this time. His parents were thrilled that we were tying the knot, and so were mine. Our wedding was a simple ceremony during the summer of 1972, in a traditional church back in Buffalo. We had our reception on the top floor of the Skateland roller skating rink immediately following the ceremony. Skateland was a rather charming establishment in the early 1970s. The top floor had a large reception hall with beautifully polished wooden floors, and there was lots of room for guests—it was the perfect setting for a wedding reception.

Every woman's wedding day should be filled with love and laughter, but for me, the most lingering memory of my first wedding is the feeling of dread that came over me while sitting next to my husband at the head table. I leaned over and said, "Let's dance." Since I'd met Billy, I'd always envisioned the two of us waltzing across some beautifully polished hardwood floors to the sounds of Duke Ellington and John Coltrane's classic "In a Sentimental Mood." Listening to Ellington repetitively ping the keys of the piano on the most popular version of that jazz masterpiece always took me to a very happy place. But my wish wouldn't come true that night. Billy turned to me with a semi-disgusted look and said, "I'm not going out there to dance." With that, he turned his back to me. No further conversation was to be had.

No new bride should have to face the harsh reality that her marriage is pretty much over while she's still entertaining guests at her wedding reception. But that's what happened to me.

This was supposed to be the most important dance of our new

life together, and he wouldn't budge from his seat. All the red flags about Billy were now waving, clear for me to see. How could we ever survive as husband and wife?

I rushed into the bathroom and sobbed for a good five minutes. In the weeks that followed, I never picked up the professional wedding pictures. What bride would only pick up the eight-by-ten wedding picture of herself and leave the rest? Well, I did.

~

I was saved from a great deal of marital discord by my continuous work and travel. Eileen Ford kept me working hard and often, though Billy hated every minute of it. He complained all the time about my long working hours, but never found the need to secure permanent employment for himself. He hated more than anything else my extended out-of-town trips, particularly those that took me out of the country. He would beg me not to leave every time I began to pack my bags. I would cry for hours before the cab showed up, while Billy would just stand there pleading with me to stay. Ultimately, our standoffs ended the same exact way: I would wipe away my tears, then jet off into the sunset.

At some point, Billy and I moved out of his parents' apartment into our own place in Brooklyn. Billy continued to halfheartedly take odd jobs here, there, and everywhere. None of them added up to much, and they paid even less. After accompanying me on one of my photo shoots, he even charmed his way into working as a photographer's assistant. It didn't hurt matters that Billy could supply all the party favors (i.e., weed) at the photo shoot, which made for an extremely happy time for all. I certainly enjoyed smoking weed in moderation, but I was becoming increasingly uneasy with the overlap of Billy's illegal gigs with my professional life. Who knew how it could affect my potential business ventures in the fashion world and beyond? But I bit my tongue and continued to pretend all was well. Love can be blind, but I knew Billy was both the best thing in my life and in some ways the worst.

To keep my spirits up and my mind focused, I met with Eileen and her team regularly to discuss my future. Eileen and I would have lunch to go over every last detail of my contracts and business deals. I loved the way her brain was wired and appreciated the time she took with me, advising me on my plans for books, movies, and countless other ventures.

But it would be a painful process. Eileen Ford and I would share a number of successful moments during the span of my career, but she didn't arrive at the top of the modeling management profession during the fifties and sixties by being a demure, meek, mild little woman. She was, even by her own account, callous, abrasive, and at times, intentionally mean-spirited to those she worked with.

Stories detailing Ford's heart of stone run rampant in the fashion industry and for good reason. Although I had heard any number of horror stories about Eileen and her rather unpleasant behavior, I never expected to have my own nightmare tales to add to the legend. But I would.

In my constant hustle for more insight into what made the Ford Agency so dominant, I would sometimes go into the offices just to hang out when I wasn't working. I chatted up various agents about who was doing what, which models were getting booked for which jobs, and who was putting on too many pounds or doing too many drugs. The more I hung around the offices, the more I learned— what I had to do to soar and, equally important, what I needed *not* to do if I wanted to gain the top spot.

On one particularly sunny morning I got more than I bargained for when I heard Eileen inside her office asking in her most frustrated voice, "Has anyone heard back from Naomi Sims?"

At the time, Naomi Sims was the most prominent African-American model in the world. Naomi had been the first woman of color to really turn fashion industry heads, in the late sixties and early seventies. But word was spreading that the trailblazing beauty was becoming more and more undependable, showing up late or not at all for photo shoots and runway shows. This had not been typical behavior displayed by her in the early stages of or even at the height of her career. Sadly, Sims was in the midst of a real-life emotional crisis that few knew about. The full extent of her struggles, which included bipolar disorder, wouldn't be understood until her death some thirty years later.

The Ford Agency sponsored an annual modeling competition in Capri, Italy, that showcased beautiful women from all around the world. Naomi always competed and was one of the few black models, if not the only, featured in the event. She was also a Capri favorite, which was no surprise, given how much Italian men love women with darker skin tones. But now she was missing.

At this point in my career, and my life for that matter, I hadn't traveled out of the state of New York, much less the country. But if Eileen saw my brown face, maybe she would realize how easily I could sub for Naomi. It wouldn't do for me to just go in and suggest the idea to her; that would be too forward and suggestive. Eileen needed to visualize on her own how perfect a fit I would be for the wonderful Naomi. After about fifteen minutes of ever so subtly inching closer to Eileen's office, our eyes met, and I could see the lightbulb go off in her head.

By that same afternoon, I was on my way to Buffalo via train in search of my birth certificate to apply for my first passport.

My traveling companions for the weeklong trip to Italy for the competition would be Eileen, her husband Gerard, and several other models. Staff members from the Ford Agency in the States, as well as other models from Ford's international offices, would join us as well.

Italy, including the island of Capri, was everything I ever imagined it would be. It was charming and beautiful. I remember wishing Dada and my sisters were there with me because there was no way I could explain to them what I was seeing. Capri was full of imperial villas, medieval churches, and elegant nineteenth-century residences. I couldn't take my eyes off the shimmering blueness of the Mediterranean Sea as we crossed over from Naples to Capri by ferry. I had never seen water that gorgeous shade of cobalt blue before.

We were all handed money by the agency to spend for the week. I don't recall the exact amount, but it was a pretty nice sum—enough to buy trinkets for loved ones back home. Holding on to that wad of cash wouldn't be easy as I walked the lovely cobblestone streets of the island. Each day was a new adventure, and I welcomed it with open arms. We visited the legendary Piazzetta, a tiny square with panoramic views, delightful pavement cafés, and exclusive boutiques. I couldn't get enough of the food of Capri. Each night everyone from the agency dined on yummy dishes with names I couldn't pronounce like *Ravioli caprese*, *Bucatini alla Chiummenzana*, and *Totani e Patate*. We were having a ball and paying little attention to our dwindling funds as we partied the week away. As I expected, the locals embraced me—and my brown skin—assuring me wherever they saw me that I would surely win the competition hands down. Anytime this happened, Eileen would chime in and quickly disagree. She wanted to make sure my hopes weren't too high. But I wouldn't let Eileen rain on my parade no matter how much she tried.

On the day of the event I rocked my *Star Wars* Princess Leia look (before there was a *Star Wars* or a Princess Leia) with my hair parted down the center and a braided bun on each side. I wore a one-piece black swimsuit with gold trim as opposed to the traditional two-piece swimsuits most of the other girls wore. (I've always been flat-chested, so two-piece bikinis didn't do much to flatter my figure.) The city turned out in full force that night, and I can still feel how my heart pounded each time I stepped onto the stage and heard the deafening applause. Even with all that, I came in second place, and the crowd began to loudly boo as I approached the stage to accept my award, which included a one-hundred-thousand-dollar one-year work contract. For a brief moment I thought they were booing me personally, until someone explained that they were booing because I had only won second place. As she handed me the trophy, Eileen said snidely, "An American had to be among the winners somehow, I guess." She had to get in a dig, but I didn't care.

My roommate, Ann, and I decided to make the most of our last days on the island and do whatever we wanted. I bought a few gifts for family and friends, which left me completely out of cash. On the night before we were to leave, Eileen gave us the exact time and place where we were all to meet up with her the next day, since she had our tickets for the ferry and flight back to New York from Rome.

In the morning, Ann and I packed and hurried down from our hotel to the villa where Eileen was staying with her husband. On our way, the cleaning ladies stopped us and told us in broken English that the guests were already gone. Alarmed, we ran to the pier, thinking Eileen and the crew would be waiting for us.

There was no one there.

The men in charge of the ferry that was idling in the bay weren't interested in giving us a free ride, so I ran up to the ferry office to find out if Eileen had left our tickets there. No luck. None of this made sense. Where could they be, and why wouldn't they leave our tickets if they went on without us?

I would have more questions and an even larger surprise when I returned to the pier minutes later. Both Ann and the ferry were gone now, too. What in the hell was going on? I immediately started looking in the water and around the pier thinking that heffa Ann had better well be floating in the ocean because she had no business leaving me like that. And the heffa had my trophy with her, too! Who did she think she was? I had given her my trophy because I didn't have enough room in my suitcase. I really didn't know what to do next. I was in a foreign country where I didn't speak the language, and I didn't have a dime to my name, or any way to get home. I didn't see how it could get much worse. I had been the toast of the town a few days before, and now I was walking the streets with my luggage, hoping to find someone who spoke at least a smidge of English so I could tell them of my pitiful plight.

Tired and hungry, I stopped by a sidewalk café and casually began chatting with a woman who spoke a bit of English. She was Angel Number 1, a wealthy woman who owned her own small plane. She was headed to Naples that day and offered me a ride. Once at the train station in Naples, I still needed to get to Rome, where the American Embassy was located. I walked up and down the platform sharing my tragic story with the workers there, but they either weren't buying it or didn't understand me.

Finally, one older gentleman—Angel Number 2—motioned for me to follow him to the back of the train. There, he slid a door open and out came the overwhelming smell of manure. Inside the train car were goats and the workers entrusted with taking them from farm to farm. The man nodded for me to get in, which I reluctantly did. I really needed the ride. I smiled sweetly at the old women and men already on board and sat down on my luggage. It took a long time to get from Naples to Rome.

A few hours into the trip, I began to smell something other than manure—the amazing aroma of spices and dough. One of the older ladies smiled and handed me a large piece of bread. It was the most delicious thing I'd ever tasted in my life, and I ate it like I hadn't eaten in a month. Angel Number 3 had appeared.

Once I arrived in Rome, I headed straight to the embassy, where they rushed through the paperwork for my ticket home. Thankful for their help and too ashamed to ask for more, I didn't have the heart to request the bus fare to the Rome airport. Dragging my luggage from the embassy to the bus stop, I finally broke down in tears; the burden of my long journey had at last taken its toll. Tears were rolling down my face as I watched person after person board the buses heading to the airport. As I stood there, I noticed a blond man staring at me. He was tall and quite good-looking, with a very cute smile. My Angel Number 4 had just arrived in the form of a German soldier. He asked me why I was crying, and I explained my situation as best I could. Amazingly, he bought me a bus ticket and we talked the entire ride. Well, I talked the entire ride and he listened; I don't think he understood the bulk of what I was saying, but he seemed to enjoy it. We parted ways with a hug just inside the airport, and I remember thinking how funny it was that some people come into our lives for a season and then some come in for just a twenty-minute bus ride. Both can make an incredible difference in your life.

That long flight back to New York gave me ample time to prepare for my confrontation with those responsible for my nightmare from hell. I took a taxi home from the airport and borrowed money from my doorman to pay for it. I barely slept that night because I was so angry.

I strode into the Ford Modeling Agency bright and early the next morning, ready to give the great Eileen Ford every part of a good tongue lashing. When I arrived, I could see her sitting inside her huge office already doing business, and I made a beeline that way. She wasn't surprised to see me at all and just sat there as I recounted the horrors I experienced at her hands. Who did she think she was, leaving me stranded alone in Italy? After I finished telling my story, she said, "That will teach you to not spend all your money when you go out of town, won't it?"

And with that, Ms. Eileen Ford picked up the phone and signaled to me that our conversation was over. This was the real world of big business and modeling. There would be no apologies or hugs to make it all better. Clearly I either had to put on my big-girl panties or pack my bags and go back home. Either way, Eileen wasn't concerned because she was Eileen Ford, and nothing I said or did that day was going to change that fact.

Still stunned, I walked out to see Ann, who was in the office, attempting to give my trophy to my booking agent. I walked right up to her and said, "What the hell happened to you?"

"Oh, did you just get back?" Ann said, with a fake laugh. "I got back two days ago. I just told those men on the ferry that I was getting on and they weren't going to put me off."

I can't even remember the rest of what she said. It was all a lie, so I just stood there and pretended to be listening. After she finished saying whatever she said, I simply walked away without so much as a good-bye. It was clear Ann wasn't going to own up to her part in my nightmare. At least Eileen was up front with her lack of remorse. Ann and I were never very friendly again after the incident. I've given a lot of thought to the real reason Eileen left me on that island that day, and the only one I can think of was to teach me a lesson. She wasn't happy that I'd won even second place in the contest or with the fact that I'd received as much attention as I did. She left us that day out of pure spite and nothing more.

In 2012, I shared my Italian story during Eileen's ninetieth birthday celebration. The room was filled with her family, friends, and beauty-industry people from around the world. The story was a real hit with everyone in the room except Eileen and her family, who did not seem amused. In hindsight, I'm not sure that was the most appropriate place or time to tell that story. My intent had been to be funny and reflective, not cruel or mean-spirited, but I didn't fully realize the hurtful impact it would have on her or her family that night. As for me, that one incident changed me and opened my eyes to all that was to follow in my modeling career, both good and bad. I was never blindsided in my career the same way again.

CHAPTER 7

Naomi

The first time I ever saw the face of Naomi Sims was on a flight from Buffalo to New York City. Naomi graced the cover of *Life* magazine in 1969, and I can still remember sitting on the plane and just staring at her image, captivated by every feature of Naomi's perfectly chiseled, mahogany-hued face. Never in my life had I seen such striking bone structure or a beauty so real and raw. From that very moment Naomi's influence on me was so profound that I began to wear my hair pulled back in a bun just as she wore hers on that *Life* cover.

Once I began to model, Naomi was one of those names I heard mentioned with equal parts awe and reverence by those in the industry—and for very good reason. Once she emerged on the fashion scene, she shattered long-standing racial barriers with just one flick of her stiletto heels.

I never thought in a million years that Naomi would take me under her wing when I started modeling, but she did. Shortly after we first met, Naomi invited me to an impromptu soiree at her home.

That was Naomi Sims at her very core: warm and wonderful from the start. Just like my dear friend Halston, Ms. Naomi loved throwing talk-of-the-town, glamorous dinner parties whenever the spirit hit her. And, boy, did I love attending them. She and her husband lived in one of the most lavish and chic apartments on the Upper West Side of Manhattan. She never failed to show kindness toward me at every turn, and as a result I mistakenly used her loving and friendly nature as the measuring stick for others in the business. It would turn out to be a big mistake.

That first night, though, inside her exquisitely decorated home, Naomi led me by the hand and personally introduced me to every guest in attendance. Now, that's what I call class. This was around 1973, and my career was really taking off. Naomi was still Queen of the Runway, but I was closing in rapidly as the new It Girl of magazine layouts. We were in different worlds, really, with, as I've said, print modeling considered a step above runway. Still, I often wondered how Naomi really felt about me during that period, though I didn't dare ask.

—

I'd already had my share of run-ins with a few other models of color and didn't want a repeat performance. There were other brown models who were none too pleased with my success and found their own ways of letting me know about it. Pat Cleveland, the life of Halston's parties, had no problem letting me know how unhappy she was with my newfound fame in print. Pat had no intention of sharing the runway mantle with me. A mixture of black, Cherokee, and Irish, the five-foot-ten native New Yorker perfected the art of walking the runway with a dance-like prance. Pat never crossed over to print magazines, something I'm sure she desperately wanted and resented me for doing. She acted as a muse for the likes of Halston, Stephen Burrows, and Yves Saint Laurent, and I was utterly fascinated by how she did whatever it was she did. However, we never shared a particularly warm relationship until well after we both retired from the modeling world. Pat never reached out to me in the way Naomi did, and I always worried that her ultimate goal was to undermine me somehow.

I had plenty of good reasons to feel that way about Pat. I remember a runway show where we were set to pass each other on the catwalk. It had been synchronized to a tee and Pat was set to go out first. I can still see her in that long chiffon dress with the billowy sleeves (Pat was always about the drama). It was decided she would walk down the catwalk with her arms outstretched. On her return up the walk, Pat was supposed to lower her arms so I could pass. Well, Ms. Pat had other ideas in mind that day. As I stood at the head of the stage before walking out, I could see her coming toward me with her arms still outstretched defiantly on either side, and all I could think was, This bitch ain't gonna let me pass!

I knew I couldn't just freeze on the stage, but I had to do something to avoid looking foolish. Being an athlete in high school meant I was quite agile, so without skipping a beat I walked down the catwalk as confidently as I could and then quickly ducked under Pat's outstretched arms. The audience roared with applause, probably assuming that our little dance had been part of the plan all along.

The lack of connection during our careers was sad for any number of reasons but mostly because of the very obvious one. We were among just a handful of high-profile women of color who worked with any consistency in the modeling world, so who had time for that mess? It was Pat, Naomi, and me out there doing our thing in the very white world of Madison Avenue. The kind of foolishness Pat had going on was just plain silly and childish as far as I was concerned. But that's not to say that I didn't understand it a little bit. From her viewpoint, I was just a browner face on the scene, prepped and primed to go, and there were only a few jobs available for people who looked like us. The industry had effectively brainwashed Pat to believe that there could be only one of us at the top of the modeling mountain at a time. Sadly, her attitude toward me wouldn't be a unique one as I continued my journey through the world of high fashion. I would face similar situations with a number of other models of color, particularly one African beauty with a penchant for marrying iconic rock stars.

~

If it sounds like I'm judging Pat harshly, let me be clear that I would never knock anyone else's hustle in this life. There has never been a guidebook available that taught black models how to maneuver through the very rocky terrain we all had to face. You simply had to follow your instincts, and I just couldn't undermine another person in the business, much less someone who looked like me. No job was worth compromising my principles.

The most memorable piece of advice Naomi Sims offered me was to avoid anyone who seemed to pit us against each other. She knew the game and wanted no part of it, and she wanted me to sidestep it as well. This piece of common sense was something I shared with all the girls who came along long after Naomi Sims left the game. Naomi's grace would cross my mind again when my moments of friction moved from Pat and on to Iman much further down the road.

Years later, I would have a heart-to-heart talk with Tyra Banks and Naomi Campbell about this topic. The two popular models began having serious issues with each other at the height of their careers. They weren't getting along and each felt undermined by the other when it came to getting the best jobs. By chance, I had gotten them in my car at the same time when they were both babes in the game, and I told them about my problems with Pat Cleveland. I then made it clear to them that there was more than enough fame and glory to go around in the world of fashion, no matter who might have told them otherwise. I also told them about Naomi Sims, who had long retired by this time. I wanted them to know how Naomi always offered me nothing but kindness when I entered the business. My point was to show these younger models that this industry wasn't a competition.

Life was hard enough, and women, whether in the modeling world or not, tend to be particularly hard on one another for the most trivial of reasons. I don't know if we're even aware most of the time that we're attacking one another. I'm just as guilty of it as the next woman and take full responsibility for whenever I've been ungenerous.

Whenever I tell anyone about Naomi Sims, an image of our first meeting always comes to my mind.

We were behind the stage of my very first Halston runway show, and I was hovering in a corner, trying as best as I could to apply my makeup. Editorial and magazine shoots were very different from runway shows back then. Magazine shoots provided hair and makeup for models so that they'd look their best. Runway shows, on the other hand, gave you only the bare essentials, because runway shows were all about the designer, so models were essentially on their own.

I hadn't done much runway modeling at this point, and no one had time to help me that day. I couldn't much blame them, given that Naomi Sims, the undisputed star of the show, was running late as usual. On the other side of the room, I could clearly see Halston pacing the floor, chain-smoking and cursing under his breath.

Suddenly, Naomi flew in and the room fell silent. The six-foot-tall model stood statue-like in the middle of the floor with her arms outstretched while attendants rushed to undress and then re-dress her.

At some point, Naomi noticed me in the corner fumbling to add another layer of blush to my cheeks and motioned for the dressers to stop. She walked over to me—in her underwear no less—and leaned down to hug me. Then, this flawless example of a woman, who had set the standard for black beauty, and all beauty, looked me straight in the eye and said, "I'm so proud of you. I see your pictures in the magazines, and all your work is so wonderful. I'm so happy for all your success! I wish you so much more. Keep up the good work!"

With that she turned to finish dressing for her moment in the Halston spotlight.

There were no elevated runways in the early seventies; models just circled the room for buyers and spectators to get a good look at the designer apparel, and whatever Ms. Naomi modeled, buyers bought and consumers wore.

Naomi was pure magic in those moments, captivating the audience with her fluid moves and limber turns. Unfortunately, she rarely had the chance to display that same magic between the pages and on the covers of high fashion publications. Though she'd graced the cover of *Life* magazine in 1969, major upscale fashion magazine covers were few and far between. While I would have great future success on the front of ritzy fashion magazines, Naomi was often passed by.

It broke my heart that Naomi never got the same cover opportunities I did, but I honestly think she may have just been too striking for the camera and the industry overall when she first hit the scene. Her presence was commanding, her teeth were blindingly white, and she had facial symmetry women willingly paid surgeons thousands upon thousands of dollars to replicate. Naomi was the epitome of womanhood from head to toe, and that can be one intimidating trait to have in a world where insecurities run amok and fuel a billion-dollar beauty industry. Simply put, she was a freak of nature.

But even before I'd met her, Naomi Sims had made an impression on me.

One brisk fall October day while I was still working at Jax's, Korby had sent me to pick up lunch near West Fifty-Seventh Street. As I made my way up the block, I noticed a small crowd gathering. I pushed my way through to catch a glimpse of what all the commotion was about. Well, the commotion was all about Naomi Sims. The undisputed Queen of the Runway was walking down the block clad completely in white. This was one of her signature looks—she donned an all-white winter wardrobe as soon as the temperatures dropped below fifty degrees. She favored that color because of the stunning way it highlighted her beautiful dark skin tone. One piece of clothing I always adored of hers was this beyond-stylish off-white wool cape. It was so drop-dead gorgeous that whenever she draped it around her six-foot frame, people literally stopped in their tracks and watched her walk down the block.

This was one of those days. Naomi was walking down West Fifty-Seventh, totally oblivious to the string of admirers she was leaving in her path. I bought my own wool cape soon after because that's how much I felt the need to be like Naomi. Friends talked me out of purchasing a cape of the same cream color, and I instead scooped up a purple cape I felt complemented my skin tone a bit better.

That wasn't the only trick of the trade I would borrow from Naomi. As black women, we often take it upon ourselves to play around with our makeup and hair products simply because we have no other choice. No one understood this reality more than Naomi. She was always whipping together some kind of cream or potion for her face and body to make her look even more stunning. This was the perfect lead-in to the makeup and wig company she would one day found after her departure from modeling. One unique formula Naomi eventually shared with me combined iodine with baby oil to give the face a reddish glow. She always wore this beautiful bronze, reddish concoction in lieu of foundation. I know it sounds a bit odd and oily, but trust me it worked well for Ms. Naomi. I put my own twist on the formula and began using the same ingredients, but only applied it to certain areas of my face that I wanted to highlight.

As our careers intersected, I put a lot of thought into where Naomi's path differed from mine. I think our different skin tones played a major role in how our careers turned out. Naomi's complexion was much darker than mine, and in the world of fashion, and more specifically fashion photography, that made a world of difference.

The art of lighting darker skin tones—to ensure that their beauty was truly reflected on glossy magazine pages—wasn't given much attention before the early seventies. There wasn't much reason to do so because models of color were rarely used in high fashion before then. Women of color hired in the early sixties usually had very light complexions and strong European features.

Naomi, in all her deep-mahogany glory, appeared on the scene during the mid-sixties, just in time for the arrival of Angela Davis and her massive 'fro, the Black Power movement, and the emergence of the Black Panthers. Perfect timing for those smart enough to understand what it meant to the world generally, but most in the fashion and beauty industry didn't get the memo.

I can't really imagine the kind of disappointment Naomi must have felt during that time in her career. I can't imagine what she thought about reaching a certain level of success in her modeling career, only to find herself unable to ascend any higher due to cultural ignorance and racial prejudice. To her credit, if those major disappointments in her career caused her any sleepless nights she never mentioned them to me. Whenever we'd see each other in the years that followed, Naomi would give me her signature long hug and congratulate me on all my accomplishments in the business.

I enjoyed the bond I had with Naomi Sims and hated it when, in the mid-seventies, her appearances became less and less frequent in runway shows and in ads. My biggest fear was that her absence was partially related to me and my continued success in the fashion game. At the time, I told myself that maybe she'd had enough of all the comparisons and the talk of there being enough room for only one brown girl at a time. The two of us had had the conversation about ignoring talk meant to pit us against each other, but had it all finally become too much for her? That kind of negative chatter was always within earshot at photo shoots and runway shows, and it could eat you up inside if things weren't going your way. But as much as I worried about Naomi and her feelings, I never asked her about it, because how honest could she have been with me? How honest would I have been if the roles were reversed?

As the years passed, I decided it wasn't my presence that led her away from modeling at all. Naomi married a very wealthy man and began building several hair and makeup businesses that thrived well into the eighties. She created the original blueprint for Iman, Tyra, Naomi Campbell, and me to brand our own images beyond being just pretty faces between, or on, the covers of magazines. I felt so honored when Naomi Sims called me and asked if I would appear in a number of ads for her beauty products

As the months turned into years and then decades, I would see my mentor only sporadically around New York as her business ventures began to wane and her public appearances became virtually nonexistent. Still, there is no chance of my forgetting the last time we saw each other in person. It was during Oprah Winfrey's Legends Ball held at her spectacular Montecito, California, home in 2005. The three-day celebration honored twenty-five African-American women in art, entertainment, and civil rights. Coretta Scott King, Diana Ross, Maya Angelou, and other women of note were honored as Legends. Many others were in attendance. Although I can't take full credit for Naomi's invitation, I often praised her publicly, including to Oprah and everyone around her. My goal was to make sure Naomi was included at all major events such as the Legends Ball and to encourage continued recognition for all her many contributions to the world of fashion. For reasons I never really understood, Naomi rarely got the attention she deserved for all her accomplishments, and that hurt my heart so much. I felt it was my duty to right that wrong any way I could. Oprah, being Oprah, loved hearing about Naomi's trailblazing work and immediately sent an invite Naomi's way. The Queen of Daytime Talk did more than just invite Naomi, she honored her as one of the 25 Legends, which I really think overwhelmed Naomi. She seemed truly grateful for all of the attention that weekend.

I think what connected me with Oprah was very much what connected me with Naomi. In Oprah, I felt the same kindred spirit I felt with Naomi. I could see someone traveling on an uncharted path, all the while preparing a road for the next generation to follow, to allow them to shine even brighter than the generation before. For that very reason, Oprah and I have shared a long and warm relationship that goes all the way back to her reporting days in Baltimore. When she first requested an interview with me in the very early eighties, my small inner circle of friends thought an interview with her would be a complete waste of my time because she wasn't working on a national show, but I strongly disagreed. I have always been honored when anyone had any interest in me or my journey over the years. No one is obligated to care about you or your accomplishments, so I have never taken a request for an interview lightly and pray I never will. I happily accepted the invitation to talk to the woman with the unique name.

During that first interview, Oprah and I strolled down West Fifty-Seventh Street together, discussing my career and the fashion world in general. We handed the microphone back and forth as we laughed and walked. Not to pat myself on the back too much, but I don't mind saying that I knew soon after meeting her that Oprah was destined to be the next big thing in television. The way she took charge of the interview that day made it clear to me that this lady had serious staying power in the entertainment industry. Oprah had an unmistakable sparkle and a forceful drive that were apparent to me from the first time we shook hands. What she wanted she got, and what she wanted was a national daytime talk show. You know the rest of the story.

What I love and still always admire about Oprah is her immense loyalty to those who were there for her from the beginning. When she became a household name with her award-winning daytime show, she often invited me on as a guest, a thank-you of sorts for that day on the streets of Manhattan. I appeared on *The Oprah Winfrey Show* twelve times, which was a godsend for me as my career transitioned from magazine covers to my own business ventures in beauty and television.

So I was in "sista-girl heaven" at Oprah's palatial mansion on that beautiful day in 2005, at the beginning of the Legends Ball weekend. Maybe because it had been such a long time since I had been in her presence, I didn't immediately recognize Naomi. She looked amazing as always and relatively the same as she had that day at the Halston show so many years before—still, something was just a bit off. Naomi was only four years my senior, but she always seemed so much more worldly, wise, and mature than me. I think it was because she began modeling when she was fifteen years old and she had seen so much more of life than I had by the time we met. I would learn much later that day at Oprah's house that Naomi was battling a form of cancer that would take her life just four years later.

Naomi Sims was also struggling with bipolar disorder. Apparently, this disease hit her hard while she was still in the modeling business and was the ultimate reason behind her many late arrivals for photo shoots, her disappearances, and her early retirement. It explained so much about her withdrawal from public life for long periods of time and the fact that she never developed extended and meaningful relationships in the industry. Seeing her at Oprah's home was the last opportunity I had to speak with my gorgeous mentor, the last time I had the chance to laugh and talk about funny moments of days gone by. The next call I received about Naomi came from her family to inform me of her death.

Her passing was sad, but the circumstances surrounding her funeral in Manhattan in 2009 were even sadder. Only about twelve people, including her children, were in attendance.

As I sat in the pew at the church with my dear friend Deborah Gregory—whom I modeled with in Europe, and who wrote the popular children's book series *The Cheetah Girls*—I was so angry that so few people turned out to celebrate the life of such a legendary and game-changing beauty. Why weren't more industry people of every color there showing respect for her life's contributions? Where were the designers with whom she worked? Where were the African-American magazine editors and beauty writers who knew her story and struggle all too well? Where were all the brown and black models (both young and old) who surely knew the story of how this woman opened—no, kicked down—doors for them? And I knew they knew the story because I had told it to them! (For the record, former models Alva Chin and Coco Mitchell attended, as did *Essence* magazine's Mikki Taylor and former editor-at-large of *Vogue* André Leon Talley.)

My heart broke, thinking of all those fake people who had jumped through hoops just to get into every one of Naomi's invitation-only cocktail parties at her home. But on her final day, they couldn't make the time to utter one last farewell.

Naomi taught me many valuable lessons while she lived, but none were as essential or as painful or as true as the one she left me in her death.

"Enjoy your life. Toot your own horn while you can, because in the end you die alone." Harsh, I know, but ultimately as real and as honest as it gets.

That's one lesson that stays with me to this day. Thank you, my dear Naomi.

CHAPTER 8

"Sex, Drugs, and Rock and Roll"

Two years into my professional modeling career, I had become an incredibly big name among the fashion elite in a relatively short period of time, but sometimes I had to ask myself if success had come at too steep a price.

By my own measure, I was missing out because I hadn't been able to acquire many of the precious things I'd always imagined I would have by my early twenties. I didn't have the "perfect" life my friend Dada had—kids, the picket fence, and a beautiful white house with the powder-blue shutters to match. That safe and serene life was everything I yearned for some days. My face had appeared in a few top magazines, and I'd traveled to some amazingly beautiful places, but I had also had to ride in back of a train filled with goat manure. Celebrity wasn't all about champagne and roses.

But I was grateful for the life I was living because I knew it was truly out of the ordinary. I was accomplishing something few women of color ever had a chance to, and I never took that for granted, even if the enormity of it all was sometimes overwhelming. There were just days when I wanted it all to slow down for a few hours, so I could exhale and, as clichéd as it may sound, catch my breath. I wanted to be a "regular" girl. I didn't feel that way about my life every day, just as I assume Dada probably didn't dream of being somewhere other than living in her white house with the picket fence in Buffalo. But I'm sure she had her days, too.

Nothing convinced me more of my new semi-fabulous reality than the day I was headed down the escalator in Bloomingdale's in Manhattan at the same time that my old pal, Jackie Kennedy, was coming up the escalator on the other side. Jackie very politely waved to me and said in a loud voice, "Hi, Beverly."

You know you've arrived when Jackie acknowledges *you* first in a public place.

While Jackie's public shout-out said something about my current station in life, I actually gauged my success in other ways. The mere fact that I was constantly booked for editorial layouts by some of the top magazines the world over said a lot; appearing regularly in *Vogue*, *Cosmopolitan*, and *Glamour* was now my job, and that was no small feat.

~

But in other areas of my life, things were not going so well. My marriage to Billy was at the top of that list.

We had been husband and wife for eighteen months, and Billy still wasn't working—well, not at a job where he was able to fill out a W-2 form. Making matters worse was how comfortable he seemed with this totally lopsided arrangement. My husband was quite content to live off my earnings for as long as I was content to allow him to do so. He broke my heart piece by piece every day for those eighteen months, and I was much too embarrassed to let anyone know what was really going on in our marriage.

I didn't have the heart to tell my mother, or even Dada, that I had known on my wedding day I was making a mistake by marrying Billy. If I had been honest with myself I would have admitted that I was blinded by his charming nature from day one. Billy was so good-looking and smart, but what did it matter if he wouldn't put any of it to use? This was the early seventies, just as the seeds of another brilliant black art form—hip-hop and rap—were being planted in New York City. I could have imagined Billy using his smarts to land at the forefront of that movement, but that wasn't in the cards, and sadly neither was the continuation of our marriage.

As I began to mourn what I realized was the start of the end of our union, I began seeking new, nonromantic relationships to fill the emotional void. That wasn't an easy task given the insane number of work hours I put in going from job to job. Editorial shoots often had a call time in the wee hours of the morning and would continue throughout the day until all hours of the night.

To help me through those times, I started to gather an array of interesting gal pals, gay friends, and characters of all types from inside my work world. Many of my nearest and dearest gal pals from those years remain in my life today, which is a rarity given that fashion is filled with big egos.

Fortunately, Lisa Taylor, Rosie Vela, Patti Hansen, and Grace Jones entered my life around this time. All these women were strikingly beautiful, and each modeled at one point in her career. Each would leave her own unique thumbprint on my life.

Patti Hansen and I had some pretty crazy, sexy, and very cool times during our photo shoots and magazine assignments over the years. Watching her fall in love with Keith Richards was both scary and incredibly fun. Patti grew up so fast once she met Keith. Nothing can prepare you for the wild antics you witness while hanging out with the Rolling Stones, just as nothing can prepare you for witnessing the notoriously cheap Mick Jagger excuse himself just before the waitress brings the check for dinner.

I loved it when I had the chance to fly on the Concord with Patti and the Stones. Keith would often play a new song for me and then wait like a little kid for my opinion. He truly valued my musical ear and knew I'd give him my honest thoughts. He will forever be the talented, cool, rocker guy.

Mick Jagger was once married to another model gal pal of mine, Jerry Hall. Long before she married him, she turned up to a photo shoot dripping in diamonds and wearing a luxurious chinchilla fur, considered by many to be the fur of furs. Jerry told us that she had been invited to some faraway Arab island for the weekend and was given the luxury goods at no charge—and nothing was given in exchange.

"I didn't even have to screw them!" she said proudly in her Texas drawl.

Jerry also told me she would ask about my joining her on the island the next time. I liked that idea—I wasn't hurting for anything, but I could always add another fur and some diamonds to the wardrobe.

A few months went by before we saw each other again, and when we did, I asked Jerry about the trip. She laughed and said when she'd showed the Arab men my photograph they had said, "She's beautiful! But she looks just like our wives, and we don't want anyone who looks like our wives."

Rosie Vela was drop-dead gorgeous, with strawberry-blond hair, and her lips were so naturally lush and full that kids teased her while she was growing up, calling her "Nigga Lips" back in her hometown of Galveston, Texas.

I kid you not, that is one of the first stories Rosie told me the day we met. I knew immediately we would become the very best of friends for life.

Rosie was so full of vigor and uninhibited fun that I loved hanging out with her. She was a real down-home Texas girl whose first passion was music. When we initially met, Rosie was in a relationship with the artist Peter Max. Max is known for his use of psychedelic shapes and bright colors in his artwork, and in the 1970s he was also heavily involved in efforts to restore the Statue of Liberty. My visits to the apartment Rosie and Peter shared on Riverside Drive were some of my most, shall we say, spiritually enlightening moments of the decade.

Peter would bring out these crazy oversized blank canvases for the three of us to paint to our hearts' desires. That little exercise released pent-up stress and anxiety I didn't know was buried deep inside me. As the night wore on, Peter would often do what many great men of that decade did—he'd bring out the good stuff so we could really paint our masterpieces in 3-D. Well, Peter painted masterpieces; ours fell way short. He offered us a little "shirt," a hallucinogen, something akin to LSD or magic mushrooms, and boy did that make our night that much more fast and furious.

Billy's side career had already introduced me to various versions of all types of drugs, so I was pretty familiar with how to manage that trippy feeling you get after taking magic mushrooms. But out-of-body experiences weren't the only perks I received when I visited Rosie and Peter. The fabulous pair also taught me something else of immeasurable value: how to eat, and when to eat.

It was absolutely an unspoken rule in the world of modeling then—as it is now—that the thinner you were the better you'd look on a page. We all lived or died by that rule and achieved it by any means we could. I remained thin by relying on any number of vices, each one more detrimental than the next. The first involved barely eating anything, all in order to maintain my 108-pound, five-foot-nine frame. I usually drank black coffee through the day to keep my energy levels up and sipped chicken broth at times to squash hunger pangs.

On one occasion my twenty-year-old body rebelled against my decision to deny it food. I was riding in the backseat of a taxicab one day, heading home from a modeling job in New York City, when suddenly, I started twitching uncontrollably. Convulsions began to take control of every inch of me as my poor cabdriver watched in the rearview mirror. I yelled at him to pull over because I knew exactly what was wrong—I had witnessed it before with other girls who weren't eating. I ran (well, wobbled) to the bodega on the corner and grabbed a bag of M&M's and devoured them. My body stopped shaking immediately, and just like that I was fine.

Now, the average person would likely reconsider her eating habits after a scare like that. But not me. To quote Tina Chow—a famous model who would one day marry Michael Chow, the owner of the famous New York eatery Mr. Chow, "Not a morsel of food shall pass these lips." I wholeheartedly agreed and would repeat that mantra daily.

I continued to barely eat until Rosie and Peter showed me the proverbial light. Once a week, Rosie would treat herself to a small bowl of brown rice and a poached egg. When I dined on that at their apartment for the first time, I thought I had died and gone to heaven. For years I was certain rice was Satan, and now I was learning I could eat brown rice once a week without gaining an ounce. I could also eat an egg once a week without gaining a pound. Why hadn't someone thought to give me this crucial information sooner? Who knows what other damage my body suffered as a result of improper nutrition during all those years?

~

Lisa was an entirely different kind of person from my other friends.

Lisa was an honest-to-goodness, true-American blue blood, and the first real one I had ever met. Her family owned a mega textile empire and had more money than the Rockefellers and the Gettys put together, or so it seemed. On most days, Lisa appeared not to have one care in the world, and why would she with a pedigree like that? She was completely fascinating and absolutely adorable. But nothing is ever as it appears, and I would later realize Lisa's happy-go-lucky persona was a façade. Still, the two of us had some kick-up-our-heels good times before some real hard truths came crashing down around us.

One of our first few outings together was to pose for the re-spected German-Australian photographer Helmut Newton in Cal-ifornia. He was well known for his sexy black-and-white images, but he rarely photographed black girls, so I was pretty excited, as well as honored, to be included in one of his shoots.

Newton did his best to live up to his erotic reputation the first time Lisa and I stepped in front of his cameras in a hotel on Sunset Boulevard. He insisted we remove our tops and bras; Lisa had few inhibitions about most things, and that flowed over to disrobing for art's sake. So I relaxed and did the same.

After we completed the work part of our day, Lisa took charge of the rest of the evening by introducing me to all her famous friends—male friends mostly—and I do mean famous. Our So Cal evenings were never dull, as we were constantly being wined and dined by Dustin Hoffman, Warren Beatty, Jack Nicholson, and Robert Evans. Dustin Hoffman was my favorite because he was just so cute and always told the corniest jokes. Lisa had dated all of them at some point, and appeared more than happy to share the love had I been the least bit open to the idea of dating any of them, too.

The opportunities for adventures in the romance department were there for the taking if I had been interested, but I really wasn't. For example, Warren Beatty felt the need to test my interest after Lisa and I had dinner with him at his Hollywood Hills home. As we wrapped up the evening, Beatty coyly suggested I stay over. It wasn't that late, I wasn't that drunk, and I had a ride home. Lisa was clearly in the middle of a romantic relationship with Beatty at this time, so I assumed he was suggesting we have a threesome. I didn't know if I should be flattered or offended—or both. I hadn't gotten that type of invitation before, though I was aware they were extended all the time. Any other man would have surely received a piece of my mind after making that kind of request to my face, but this was Warren Beatty in his glory days when he was a true Hollywood movie star. In the end, I said a simple no thank you. Threesomes weren't my cup of tea, and I wasn't about to change that just to fit into the Hollywood scene or to make the admittedly adorable Warren Beatty happy for a night. (Later, though, when I thought about it some more, I realized it had been a damn insulting and outlandish suggestion.)

Though Warren Beatty was a bust, I was pleasantly surprised when Jack Nicholson arrived in New York not long afterward and called to ask me to join him for a night on the town. We went to the theater (not a clue as to what we saw that night) and had dinner afterward. Jack is both charming and entertaining as all get-out, and even then he had a reputation as a ladies' man. At the end of the evening, he politely asked me if I wanted to join him back at his Upper East Side apartment. I liked Jack, but not enough to join him back at his apartment that night, though I was flattered he asked. Without missing a beat, Jack flashed me that infamous Nicholson grin before signaling to his driver to take me home.

I didn't get a call from Jack for a second date. I sometimes wished he had called because I would have loved getting to know him better. But with so many options, famous men really have little incentive to get to know someone better. For the record, inviting a woman home after the first date is not an example of real interest from my standpoint. But I didn't hold it against Jack, and now, whenever I see him out and about in Los Angeles, he always waves at me and blows me a kiss from across the room.

Lisa was a doll for introducing me to all her famous pals—not everyone would have been so kind as to share so many big-name celebs with a friend. She had beauty, money, and access to the most famous names in the business, and I never thought twice about what might be happening in the rest of her world. I wasn't big on digging into other people's personal lives, because I sure didn't want anyone digging into mine. If someone wanted me to know something, they would tell me, and vice versa. Lisa had a lot of relationships with men, which could have signaled something deeper or nothing at all. What did I know? What I *did* know was that she would often complain about her parents' backward views on race in America. They hadn't evolved on the issue as much as she had, which seemed to bother her a great deal.

Whatever life issues Lisa was facing, I never suspected they were serious enough that she would try to take her own life.

Lisa always showed up for work—we both shared that trait. So I knew something was wrong when she missed a *Vogue* photo shoot. That just wasn't Lisa. Worried, I called Eileen Ford, and Eileen, being Eileen, went into full mama bear mode, calling the NYPD, demanding they break down Lisa's Upper East Side apartment door. That was one time I was grateful for Eileen's dominating personality. The police found Lisa just in the nick of time—she was close to death from a drug overdose. Her life saved, she entered therapy, and eventually returned to modeling, where she enjoyed a long and thriving career.

Lisa is now healthy, married with kids, and has spoken openly in several documentaries about the many personal demons that haunted her both before and during her days as a model. She emphasizes that modeling only helped magnify her struggles. Our experiences together, both good and bad, created an unbreakable bond between us that I hold very dear.

Lisa wasn't alone in her struggles with drugs. Drugs were pretty much everywhere during the seventies. Hollywood, the music industry, the fashion industry, or right up front in my soon-to-be-ex-husband's side hustle—there was no escaping the hold drugs had on that era or on my generation. The civil rights movement ended, the conflict in Vietnam was winding down, and people across the country in general appeared to be in need of a release from the heavy emotional burdens of the previous decade. Drugs fit that bill.

It was an "anything goes" time for some of us. And in my world, there was no better example of the anything-and-everything-goes lifestyle than the famed nightclub Studio 54. I only made one trip to Studio 54 in all my years in New York. That said, although I may have stepped foot into the place only once, I ended up staying three days once I got there.

If ever there were a world similar to what I thought Sodom and Gomorrah from the Scriptures would have been like, it was that legendary establishment. On the Friday I arrived, one of the club's owners, Steve Rubell, singled me out of the huge crowd outside and I walked right into the world's most famous nightspot.

The ground floor of Studio 54 had tables with servers circling around you carrying plates of anything and everything your heart desired, and I do mean drugs. Downstairs, where the bathrooms were, anything and everything you could imagine was happening. People were shooting up, snorting up, and screwing, as if they were in the privacy of their own homes. You literally would have to step over couples fornicating in the middle of the floor to get into a bathroom stall. Used condoms were stuck to the floor panels and half-naked men and women (or completely naked) walked around as if they were in the Mardi Gras parade. Cocaine was being passed around on trays.

I'd seen my share of shocking sights in the early years of my modeling career, but nothing really prepared me for what I saw at Studio 54 over the course of those three days. I understood that I wasn't dealing with reality anymore.

But I also understood the life I was living at that moment, and that I had been placed there for a reason. My goal was to reach the highest levels possible in modeling, so turning back was not an option for me. Getting what I wanted meant I couldn't always be in my comfort zone, and there were people at Studio 54 whom I needed to see.

I finally made my way up to the third floor of the club. Halston, Andy Warhol, and countless other famous faces of the day huddled there on long, cozy couches. There, these independent thinkers exchanged ideas on books, fashion, movies, plays, and whatever else brilliant minds share when they get together in one room. I felt pretty special sitting in the middle of all that. It was a big confidence booster for me to realize they wanted to hear my input.

Breakfast was ordered in for all of us, as was lunch. Then, like *Groundhog Day*, the night would begin all over again. Clothes and costumes were already there, so there was little need to go home to change. Halston, Calvin, Ralph, Diane von Furstenberg, and countless other designers who regularly called the famed nightclub their home away from home made sure an endless supply of everything guests needed was on hand. I'll never forget dragging myself into work Monday morning and hearing my hairdresser, as he pulled confetti out of my hair, say, "I know where you were the last few days."

As for drugs, you didn't have to go to Studio 54 to get your fix. In the fashion world, they were provided for us models free of charge.

I won't sugarcoat my involvement with drugs. It really came down to vanity, pure and simple. The allure of cocaine for me was initially tied directly to what I saw when I looked in the mirror. When I was using coke, the whites of my eyes seemed much clearer, my weight dropped, and the bone structure in my face became more pronounced. This is exactly the result every model wants. That's how you get roped in, and that's how you get stuck.

That's more than likely what happened to the model Gia. There is really no way to discuss this period of my life or the drugs that ran rampant in the modeling industry without mentioning Gia Carangi.

Gia was a gorgeous girl from Philadelphia, whose dark, melancholic Italian looks stood in bold contrast to the typical blond-haired, blue-eyed beauties who dominated the fashion industry back then. Gia was often a part of my group of girls, the ones regularly chosen to appear in fashion layouts together for top magazines. We all formed a pretty tight bond as a result, but Gia always remained a bit of an outsider. Friendly, but aloof, Gia was difficult to figure out, but over time the reasons behind her mysterious personality would become painfully apparent.

Gia and I shared a champion in famed photographer Francesco Scavullo. He had been instrumental in launching Gia's career and would soon play a key role in defining mine, too. It was hard not to adore Francesco because his heart was so big and so giving. Francesco was set to shoot just the two of us at his studio for a feature magazine spread, and it wasn't until he brought us together that day that I began to fully appreciate the depth of Gia's drug issues.

Gia rushed into Francesco's photo studio late and immediately asked me if I wanted to meet her in the restroom to do a quick "one and one" before our session began. (One and one is when you take a hit of cocaine in one nostril and then a second hit in the other.) Everyone in those days carried their cocaine in these cute little glass bottles that looked like petite decorative vases. In the restroom I watched in horror as Gia began to pull out a rumpled piece of aluminum foil from her handbag. In my head I thought, What is this crazy chick doing?

But Gia had another huge surprise for me that day. She wasn't carrying cocaine in her purse. She unraveled the aluminum foil to reveal something else entirely: heroin. Only then did it hit me how much trouble Gia was really in.

I had used my fair share of cocaine, but heroin was hard-core, and I knew enough at that point to run in the opposite direction of it and from anyone using it. I'm pretty sure that was the last time we ever worked together and possibly the last time I ever saw Gia.

She continued to get jobs here and there for a while after that, but eventually her drug addiction got the upper hand. Makeup artists began to complain about the extra work required to cover the track marks on her arms. Years later, we would all learn of Gia's death due to AIDS. She had moved back to Philly to live with her parents after she could no longer find work. Francesco, bless his heart, continued to send financial support her way until the end. Gia was only twenty-six years old when she died.

Gia's AIDS- and drug-related demise didn't quite have the sobering impact it should have had on the modeling industry at the time, partially because she had vanished from the scene years before her death. What was clear was that the fashion industry had the potential to crush even the best and strongest of us. Your life was often not your own, and yet everything was handed to you on a silver platter whether you asked for it or not. It sounds fun, and it can be for a time, but it can also emotionally stunt you, leaving you ill-equipped to face the future. For many, fame and fortune is a lonely journey that ends abruptly. And reality is often far away. I can recall few times when I was a top model that I scheduled a doctor's appointment, pumped gas, bought an outfit, or purchased groceries. How can you become whole and complete without those basic life experiences to draw upon? That's why I continued to yearn for and search for a sisterhood beyond my siblings and Dada. Oftentimes, I'd find that connection in the strangest places.

～

During the seventies, roller skating rinks grew to be the funkiest and most fabulous spots for the hippest parties in town. A skating rink soiree was one of the hottest tickets back then, and it didn't matter the name on the invitation, I always wanted to throw my skates on. Skating rinks have always had a special place in my heart, even before my wedding reception at Skateland in Buffalo.

One night, at one skating party in Manhattan, I was rolling along, minding my own business, when I was bumped hard from behind and almost fell to the floor. I was really mad, and it took a moment for me to regain my composure. I looked back to see who had pushed me, and there was a semi-bald, hot-pink-shorts-no-top-wearing Grace Jones!

Nothing pisses Grace Jones off more than being ignored—so I ignored her.

Grace's androgyny, her commanding voice, her crew cut, her mile-high cheekbones, her dark brown skin, and her steely stare had turned her overnight into a fashion superstar. She had walked the runways for Yves Saint Laurent and Kenzo and had become a cult figure. Her beauty was unique, and she cleverly turned her looks into a career that showcased both her singing and acting ability. I always admired a good hustle, and Grace's was among the best in the game. A true friendship between us wouldn't develop until years after the skating incident, when many of the personal demons we had both tried to sidestep could no longer be avoided.

As my list of friends expanded, so did my workload, and I needed my own glam squad to keep me ready at a moment's notice. This style and beauty crew would be exclusively in charge of making certain I appeared my best each time I stepped out in front of a camera.

Ultimately, that glam crew came down to just one man: James Farabee. I can't remember exactly how I met James. But like most black women, I was always on the lookout for a good hairstylist, which is likely how we crossed paths. You never lose the number of a good stylist, and James was practically perfect in his presentation and his craft. He had been trained in the beautification of hair and skin, and just one visit to his salon was life-affirming for any woman who sat in his chair. In those days, black skin and hair were still deep mysteries to the mainstream world of beauty professionals. The most renowned hair and makeup experts hired by most major publications for photo shoots were white and not trained to work with curly, kinky hair or darker skin tones. We black women were forced to do our own research to find our own wonder beauty products, so when I found James, it was true love from day one.

James created special concoctions at his Upper East Side Manhattan salon to make sure my skin stayed smooth and pimple free. He also created a regimen for my hair so that it would remain healthy and easy to maintain. (James even gave Eileen Ford a perm to straighten her short and frizzy mane.)

Beyond the beauty help, James also became my mentor in an entirely different level of art and culture from the one I'd known with Billy Potter. James didn't just talk culture and beauty, he breathed, lived, and created it through his work. Several nights a week, I accompanied him to performances at the American Ballet Theatre, the Alvin Ailey American Dance Theatre, and the New York Metropolitan Opera. He insisted I grow spiritually and musically by listening to the recordings of Maria Callas, Nina Simone, and Leontyne Price. And he told me it was crazy to live in Brooklyn and not in Manhattan.

James also balked at my choice of husband and often hinted that it was way past time for a relationship upgrade. His words of wisdom did ultimately push me to finally pull the plug on Billy Potter and his eighteen-month reign of foolishness in my life. The final straw was Billy's frantic call to me one day telling me of his arrest for smoking weed on the subway. Billy demanded I come immediately to bail him out of jail; I took a deep breath and calmly told my very-soon-to-be-ex-husband that I would not be coming to his rescue that night.

My career was going too well to get involved in Billy's dumb-ass antics anymore. His poor parents bailed him out of jail the next day, but not long after his subway arrest, I felt I had no other choice but to file for divorce. That said, it didn't exactly change much, since it took a while for Billy to move out of the apartment.

One day while we were lying in bed together, I told Billy that I would be finalizing the divorce papers that very morning. Billy didn't respond—in fact, he didn't say a word or even move. So I got dressed and headed to the courthouse to meet my lawyer and sign the papers. Uncontested divorces weren't very complicated, and since it was the middle of the week, I was back across the Brooklyn Bridge and at home in a matter of hours. Billy was exactly where I'd left him—in the bed, beneath the covers. Seeing him in that same position, I did what any self-respecting woman does when she has just divorced her husband. I got right back into the bed with him and we made love.

It would be months before Billy moved out of the Brooklyn apartment we shared. Even then, he would come back and stay whenever he pleased. He was my first true love and those feelings don't fade easily. Billy and I still speak today from time to time, and I kept in touch with his wonderful mother until she passed away just a few years ago. Some people, friends, and lovers come into our lives for a reason, or a season, and now both Billy's reason and season were over. He would reappear again over the years in my times of need. But at that moment, history-making events were on the horizon for me, and I had to be ready.

CHAPTER 9

"Darling, You Should Always Wear Red!"

Things changed rapidly after I ended my marriage with Billy. I moved to Manhattan, and almost immediately I landed a prime, six-week modeling assignment in Brazil. Cheryl Tiegs and I would be photographed along the Amazon. Life was good.

Brazil was wonderfully soothing to me—I fell in love with it the moment our plane touched the ground. Its festive city streets and pristine beaches pulsated with life, and the lushness and beauty was matched by the Brazilians themselves, whose varied cultures—be it indigenous Indian, Portuguese, or African—made for a fascinating melting pot.

The editors of *Vogue* had several ideas for the spread, and by far the most dramatic idea was for a gigantic snake to wrap itself around me in the rain forest while I stood perfectly still for the photo. Now, as a rule I was pretty easygoing and rarely complained or said no to the creative ideas or visions of the editors. But the idea of a large snake curling around my body was going a bit too far for my liking.

I told both the photographer and Vera Wang—who long before being a renowned haute couture wedding gown designer was a senior fashion editor at *Vogue*—that I was scared. Their plan to reassure me involved taking me to the hut of a very experienced snake owner so I could have a trial run to calm my nerves.

Our guide, who was also a journalist, took us on a boat ride down the Amazon to meet the snake trainer. As we were riding through a waterfall, I put my hand out to feel the running stream, but when the guide noticed what I was doing, he immediately told me to stop before a piranha reached out and bit my hand off. What a doll! I was slowly falling in love with our guide, who had the sexiest accent and was clearly very concerned for my well-being. He was also quite good-looking, smart, and resourceful—heck, he had two jobs, and I'd just gotten divorced from a man who didn't like the idea of holding even one.

My fear of posing with a snake was actually doubled once we reached the snake owner's straw hut and I saw the twenty-foot python in the flesh. I wanted no part of him. The *Vogue* editors, though, began spinning the tale of how if I didn't do the shoot with the snake, the poor snake owner and his family wouldn't be able to eat because the money they made from that one photo shoot would support the entire family for the year.

Who knows if that was actually true or just a damn good lie used to get me to do what they wanted me to do. Whatever it was, the guilt kicked in. The family did look pretty destitute, and I didn't want to be the one responsible for them not having enough food for the rest of the year.

The next day we took another boat ride to the area where the shoot was to take place. By this point I was officially in love with our guide, and he was in love with me from what I could tell. On the way to the shoot, we stopped to pick up the snake, and that's when we found out that the snake owner we'd met the day before wouldn't be joining us because he was in the hospital—he'd been bitten by a snake! Although not by the same snake we were using that day, apparently.

"You must be kidding!" I screamed. "I'm not doing this!"

What made it worse was that the handler's nine-year-old son would be handling the snake, but as they told me this, they also reminded me of the family-won't-eat situation, and to get them all to shut up I had to give in once again.

At the shoot, the nine-year-old kid placed the twenty-foot python around me as I lay at a forty-five-degree angle on a tree, as still as possible. As the snake slithered slowly around me, I could hear the crew oohing and aahing about how amazing the photos looked, so I gritted my teeth and kept posing for the camera. Just when I thought it couldn't get any worse, a few large spiders appeared out of nowhere to join the snake, and I was done. I told the kid to get that damn snake off me. The shoot was over—nothing else would be crawling on me that day.

We shot a variety of photo layouts during the six weeks in Brazil, but I also managed to fit in samba classes every day. I fell in love with samba, a distinctive kind of music with African roots that really took off at the beginning of the twentieth century in Rio de Janeiro. The music was strongly influenced by the immigrant population from the Brazilian state of Bahia, and it later inspired the dance that shares its name. Learning it brought me a great deal of joy.

I always enjoyed tasting the local cuisine of every country I visited during my career, too. Brazil's national dish is feijoada, a tasty stew that differs throughout the country, but where I was it comprised beans, fresh pork or beef, cabbage, kale, potatoes, okra, carrots, and pumpkin in one large yummy meal. Feijoada had been served to Brazilian slaves, because it contained the unwanted parts of the pig (such as the feet, nose, ears) and cheap black beans. This made me think of African-American slaves who were fed from the leftovers of whatever was served in the main house on the plantation.

At the six-week mark, when the crew was ready to pack their bags for departure, I decided I wouldn't follow. I was in love with João, the guide/journalist, and wanted to stay in Brazil longer to enjoy my newfound freedom, the rain forest, and him. I also wanted to keep dancing the samba! All was well until two weeks later when João was on the verge of being arrested for his antigovernment stance in a recent editorial piece he'd written for the local paper. His arrest would surely lead to my arrest, and that wasn't part of the plan. Time to move on, it seemed.

I called Eileen Ford and told her the love affair was over and that I was ready to come home. Eileen had some news that would cheer me up: another assignment. I would be heading to Greece for *Glamour* magazine, which she knew would be right up my alley. I longed to travel to Greece and see where Jackie Kennedy had once lived.

I bid João a fond good-bye and hopped on a plane to Greece. But on the trip, my stomach started doing cartwheels and my head was hurting as well. Once I landed in Greece, I began to feel worse, so I headed to my room in the hotel and got into bed. I alerted the *Glamour* staff that I was sick, and when the editors saw my condition, they arranged for a doctor to visit. I knew something was very wrong when they all began to converge outside instead of inside my room to discuss my health. The first diagnosis was cholera, but that was quickly ruled out as they determined it had to be some type of parasite that I picked up while in Brazil. After I developed a high fever and began to lose weight, they decided it was best to fly me back to New York on a private plane so that the doctors there could determine what treatment would be most effective.

I'll never forget being wheeled off that plane on a stretcher that sunny day at a small airfield just outside New York. Waiting for me were the two most important women in my life: my mother and Eileen Ford. My mother started crying the moment she saw me because I'd lost so much weight from the constant vomiting and severe diarrhea. She couldn't believe how small I was; Eileen Ford, on the other hand, was just glad I had made it back alive. Fortunately, the doctors in New York didn't take long to figure out which parasite I had, and I was back on my feet in a matter of weeks.

No one was happier to see me up and out than my beloved guru James, who thought it was high time to put my good name to use and expand my empire beyond modeling. He was now unofficially in charge of advising me about how to make the most of every ounce of my growing star status, power, and fame in the fashion game. Though he was technically my hair and skin specialist, as with many women, my hairstylist was so much more.

James had a host of plans for me that included developing a slew of beauty products we would launch together. Over the years, James had concocted his own impressive array of the most wonderful hair shampoos and conditioners made from nothing more than natural fruits and vegetables that he grew in his own home garden. He then mixed the fruits and vegetables with essential vitamins and nutrients that nourished all hair types back to their original healthy state.

With James's endless ideas for branding my image—a business idea still in its infancy at the time—he felt it was crucial that I meet with Eileen Ford to press the issue of my face becoming a cover of *Vogue* magazine in the very near future. I ran in the same circles with all those girls whose faces regularly appeared on *Vogue* covers, and I had already appeared on a number of *Glamour* magazine covers, not to mention numerous spreads inside *Vogue*. James believed that Eileen would agree that I had done enough modeling jobs to have my face on the cover of a major upscale fashion magazine, no question. The color of my skin should have no bearing at all on the decision. But I worried that the perm James applied to Eileen Ford's naturally curly/kinky hair had given him a false impression about how her brain worked.

For a start, just a few months earlier I'd had a run-in with Ms.

Eileen about fair and equal pay for models on fashion shoots, and the fight hadn't been very pleasant.

One day on a catalogue shoot, I had casually asked some of the models what they were being paid for that particular job. Some of the girls didn't like discussing money, but others were quite happy to share. When I learned how much less I was earning than some of my counterparts, I couldn't believe it. Some were getting paid almost twice as much as I was, and in some instances for less work than I was putting in.

This simply wasn't fair or acceptable. I decided not to bring race into it, though I easily could have. Right was right, and I could fight it on those merits alone.

Eileen was the first person I called when I returned home from the shoot. She already knew about the pay differences because she'd negotiated my contracts, and I told her that I wanted this unfair practice fixed. She said she would make some calls about it, and in a matter of weeks, the pay matter was resolved and I was getting paid the same amount as other models. As word spread about what had happened, several other black models also asked for equal pay on catalogue shoots, and their requests were granted as well. That ol' saying "You won't know until you ask" is so true.

It didn't occur to me at that time, but I was making a major impact on the unfair practices of an industry that generated millions of dollars each year. In a small way, I was fulfilling my childhood dream of pushing for justice!

This victory made me even more determined to talk with Eileen about getting that cover of *Vogue*. It had been a dream of mine since I first moved to New York, and my hope was that Eileen's cunning, savvy, and brilliant business mind would join me in trying to figure out a way of turning my dream into reality.

Sadly, Eileen did not share my dream. She told me point-blank that *Vogue* would not put my face on the cover. As odd as it may sound, at the time I didn't look deeper into her denial or the meaning behind her steadfast refusal to get me the cover. All I knew was that Eileen was done with the conversation and had made it clear that I needed to be done with the idea as well.

But I couldn't give up that easily on something I wanted so badly. My goal was always to become, if not *the* top model, one of the top models in the world. I couldn't do that without having a *Vogue* cover. Getting the *Vogue* cover was how you reached the pinnacle of the business back then; now, it's actresses who hope they'll get the cover, but its power is still the same.

If Eileen wouldn't assist me in getting what I wanted, I knew someone who would.

Her name was Wilhelmina (Willy) Cooper, and Eileen knew the Dutch-born beauty even better than I did. At one time, she had been the Ford Agency's most profitable supermodel; she had epitomized the classic, aristocratic look of the fifties and sixties with her swan-like neck, doe eyes, and delicate cheekbones.

Standing at five-foot-eleven, Wilhelmina was often hailed as one of the few high-fashion models in those days built like a real woman, with measurements 38-24-36. In her heyday she appeared on the cover of American *Vogue* a staggering twenty-eight times.

In 1967, Wilhelmina, along with her husband Bruce Cooper, a former executive producer of *The Tonight Show*, pulled off the ultimate coup. They formed the Wilhelmina Models agency, which offered the first real bona-fide threat to Eileen's several-decade hold over the modeling game and Madison Avenue. Eileen was furious at what she perceived to be Wilhelmina's betrayal, and to any model that dared leave the Ford Agency to sign with Wilhelmina Eileen sent a Bible with passages referring to Judas underlined in bold red Magic Marker.

Blame it on those girls from my Buffalo neighborhood who tried to jump me on a weekly basis, but I had little fear of Eileen's wrath. Her refusal to help me get the *Vogue* cover meant I had no other choice, so I reached out to Wilhelmina. Willy had assisted Naomi

Sims in her early days when no one would consider taking a chance on a dark brown girl appearing between the covers of nonblack magazines. She encouraged Naomi constantly and put her on the path to the major triumphs of her career, which included the covers of two nonfashion magazines, *Ladies' Home Journal* and *Life*.

I remember meeting the lanky former model as she sat at her oversized wooden desk eating a slice of pizza with her feet propped up and a burning cigarette in a nearby ashtray. Cigarette smoking would be the primary cause of her death just a few years later at the very young age of forty, but that day I told her my dream of a *Vogue* cover and her face lit up.

This meant parting ways with Eileen, but I would do it with as much class as possible. Eileen was the most powerful agent in the business and making an enemy out of her wasn't a very smart move. Most of the other girls who left Eileen would slither away to join another agency without giving notice, believing they were somehow wrong to act in their own best interests. But my brain didn't work like that. This was my career, so I had no fear in discussing my move face-to-face with her. There was no need for underhanded or backdoor moves on my part. I would thank her profusely for all her support and hard work on my behalf. She deserved my thanks and my honesty, and I wanted to make sure I could return if this new arrangement didn't bring the results I expected.

I was surprised at how gracious she was. Despite our disagreements over the years, I really think Eileen appreciated my honesty and gratitude, and she said she would welcome me back if I did indeed decide to return.

With Wilhelmina now running the show, I continued receiving bookings for editorial shoots in all the top magazines. In fact, my workload actually increased, because people were so shocked Eileen didn't send her "death squad" after me. There was plenty of talk around town about my defection from the Ford Agency to Wilhelmina's company, but I had become accustomed to the constant chatter about what I was doing and why. The media coverage of celebrities in 1974 wasn't as huge an issue as it is now.

While Wilhelmina was busy singing my cover-worthy praises to editors and photographers around Manhattan, I had other high-profile champions on my side, too. At one photo shoot with supermodel and part-time rebel Lauren Hutton (a lady well known for speaking her mind at all times), she bluntly told the entire editorial team that it should be me and not her getting prepped and primed for the *Vogue* cover that month. She was the great Lauren Hutton, so she knew she could say what she wanted without fear of reprisal. And she was more aware than I that *Vogue* was hesitant to put black faces on its cover.

Lauren also knew that her words would travel verbatim to every fashion editorial staff in Midtown. Not many top models in her position would have done what she did at the time. Lauren Hutton still remains a hero to me because she took a stand.

But while the Laurens of the modeling world would have major cover shoots set up for them well in advance, that wasn't how my career-defining moment played out in 1974.

~

On the day my *Vogue* cover shot was taken, I actually was on a photo shoot for the inside of *Vogue*. There was nothing out of the ordinary to suggest this shoot would be any different from any of the other editorial spreads I'd done. My beloved Francesco Scavullo was the photographer, and we were working in the location he loved the most, his Midtown home/studio. I adored his gorgeous and well-lit space as much as he did, and shooting there meant I would also get to see his adorable live-in love and assistant Sean Byrnes.

But what I appreciated most of all about that day was the fact that my face would be in the hands of a true master. Aside from his photography, he had also painted an award-winning portrait of singer Janis Joplin in 1969 just a few months before she died. He was hired to create shots for the movie posters for *A Star Is Born*, starring Barbra Streisand and Kris Kristofferson, and was commissioned by Mikhail Baryshnikov to photograph the dancers of the American Ballet Theatre.

Frances Stein, the fashion director at *Vogue*, was there, too, and she wasn't too shabby, either. The former fashion director at *Glamour*, and now second-in-command under the icon of all fashion icons, Diana Vreeland, Frances had chosen a tantalizing periwinkle-blue sweater as one of the outfits for me to wear, and it was truly a divine match next to my skin. We girls loved to call Frances "Frankenstein" behind her back.

(I had met Diana Vreeland, the grand dame of all things fashion, on just one occasion, while I was at a New York party, and I was wearing a one-of-a-kind red evening gown. Diana took one look at me and proclaimed as loudly as she could, "Darling, you should always wear red!" A legend in the fashion world and a huge personal hero of mine, Vreeland began her publishing career in 1936 as a columnist for *Harper's Bazaar*. My favorite story about Vreeland is that in 1955 she moved into an apartment that was decorated exclusively in red.)

At the shoot, Frances added a scarf to accent the neck of the blue sweater, and let me tell you no one could fool around with an accessory the way ol' Frankenstein could. She must have twisted and knotted the scarf thirty times and switched the brooch from side to side about twenty times. Patience is a must when you're a model, and Frances just about wore mine out that day with all her fiddling and fussing.

Frances and Francesco chatted back and forth, as though I weren't there, about how much they loved that vibrant burst of color on me. I was rarely photographed in colors so bold and wondered why someone hadn't thought of it before. The day was turning out to be something very special.

Also on hand to beautify me every step of the way were Way Bandy and Suga, who made up what I like to call the "crème de la crème" of stylists back in the day. Way was a Picasso of makeup, spending hours just applying my foundation with a Q-tip for a finish so seamless and natural even I couldn't tell where the makeup began and where it ended. Then there was Suga, a Japanese hairstylist who was right up there next to James as the best one in this country.

How I adored those two men with all my heart. They were such perfectionists in their craft. I would watch in awe as they performed their beauty magic: curling, stippling, and brushing. Just being in their presence and picking up tidbits from their chatter made me feel as though I could teach a master class at Parsons School of Design. (Sadly, AIDS would claim the lives of both of those beautiful men just a few years later. It broke my heart.)

What I remember so vividly about that day was that from the moment I opened my eyes, it had had a magical feel. I wouldn't understand how magical and life-altering it was until a few months later, when Wilhelmina dialed my apartment early one morning.

"Beverly, you're on the cover!"

"Of what?" I replied without thinking.

"*Vogue*, of course!"

I asked if she could please repeat those words because I wasn't sure I heard her correctly. She said it again, this time a bit slower. "You are on the August cover of *Vogue*!"

"Really" is the only word I could manage to get out of my mouth. I believe I said thank you before ending the conversation, but the memory is fuzzy all these years later.

Though I took Willy at her word, "only seeing equaled believing," as we said in my neck of the woods. I hurriedly pulled on my jeans, threw on a white T-shirt, and ran down to the local newsstand without even thinking to take my purse with me. The early morning rush in Manhattan was on, with the nine-to-five work crowd in line for their java and a newspaper. I was still too hyped to realize I had no money. When I pointed to the *Vogue* magazine featuring my face and that beautiful blue sweater styled by Frances, I knew the man recognized that it was me on the cover and was impressed, but not impressed enough to hand over the magazine for free. But at least now I had proof the cover was mine, so I took my time heading back to my apartment to pick up my wallet. On the way, I stopped by a pay phone to call my mother—collect—to tell her about the cover. I was screaming with excitement and so was she, though I doubt she understood the significance of it all.

In a matter of days my entire world changed. Though I hadn't thought much about what it would mean to be the first black woman on the cover of *Vogue* magazine, I had no choice but to seriously ponder its significance after the cover debuted.

For generations in this country, beauty was traditionally represented by three very distinct ideals in virtually all media: blond hair, blue eyes, and fair skin. Whether in movies, on television, or on magazine covers, that stereotype never deviated. My *Vogue* cover shattered that notion forever. It built an immediate bridge for a group of women who had long been invisible to mainstream beauty editors and Madison Avenue. Women of color could boldly say to the world, "Hey, look at me! I'm here and I have value and I am beautiful."

Beautiful black women had only been sporadically seen and acknowledged before the seventies. Lena Horne, Dorothy Dandridge, and Pearl Bailey had appeared in occasional film roles during the forties, fifties, and sixties. In fashion, Helen Williams and Donyale Luna had only rarely been able to model outside the confines of the traditional black magazines, *Jet* and *Ebony*.

In Africa and especially Europe, the press were the first to recognize the importance of my *Vogue* cover when it hit the stands. Magazines on those continents had already been far more likely to showcase black women's beauty, and accordingly they put in the first requests for interviews with me and highlighted the issue of race in the world of fashion and entertainment.

On the rare occasions when the beauty of black women *was* recognized in the US, the impact was often minimal. As the sixties ended and the seventies began, Cicely Tyson, Diahann Carroll, Pam Grier, Diana Ross, and Tamara Dobson were all black women with notable names enjoying a high level of visibility not seen before by women with darker hues.

Still, there was controversy surrounding many of the images depicting black women. Many felt Pam Grier's roles on the big screen were overly sexualized and reinforced stereotypes of black women present since slavery. Pam has been a longtime friend of mine, and I was happy she finally got a chance to shine in the 1997 film *Jackie Brown*, for which she was nominated for a Golden Globe Award.

The faces of Diahann Carroll and Diana Ross were less controversial, because they portrayed less racy characters, but in any case, as with Pam, audiences had to pay to see their films and listen to their albums. One of the reasons my *Vogue* cover resonated in the way that it did was because it was sold at every grocery store checkout counter around the country, and every newsstand carried a news banner that ran across the top of the stand showcasing the *Vogue* cover of the month. There was simply no way to escape my face during the month of August 1974, no way to escape what the new face of beauty might look like in the coming years. That fact alone left an enduring mark on the country, its view of beauty, and the meaning of beauty for decades to come.

It may be hard to believe today, in an age where everyone appears to have an agenda for just about everything, but it was never my goal to become the first African-American woman to appear on the cover of *Vogue*. President Barack Obama didn't campaign to become the country's first black president in 2008. He was a man who wanted to be president of the United States based on his merits and his work as a community servant. He just happened to be black.

If I'd gone to meetings with Eileen or Willy with any type of agenda, my face would never have landed the cover of *Vogue*. My reasoning for wanting the cover was connected to my deep passion for my work and the legacy I wanted to create and leave behind. My race was merely the icing on the cake.

I always wanted the distinction to be that I was a top model who also just happened to be black. I was by no means some black revolutionary fighting for racial equality. That wasn't my job, though I admired those who took it upon themselves to fight for it, and I did understand the significance of progress. Of course I appreciated how my face on the cover of *Vogue* reverberated the way it did then, and I appreciate the way it continues to have significance.

From day one the cover was described as breaking the color barrier much in the same way Jackie Robinson broke it in baseball. That was a lot to take in as a twenty-two-year-old girl from Buffalo. I was overwhelmed by the enormous honor, while at the same time frightened that I wouldn't be able to live up to what it meant. Twenty-two years old is pretty young to take in much of anything, especially what you mean to an entire race.

As proud as I was of being the first African-American model to appear on the cover, I realized I didn't know quite enough about the history of my race. To combat that, I began collecting books on African history, the slave trade, and the early years of Africans on American soil. My parents hadn't taught any of us much about our African past, and the school system hadn't done much better. (In fairness, my mother and father hadn't been taught much by their parents or teachers, either.) And you can't teach what you don't know.

What I didn't want to do was to sit in an interview and be asked a question regarding black history that I couldn't answer. Fortunately, right before the cover appeared I'd hired a publicist, and she sometimes stepped in when it appeared I might be oversharing my opinions during interviews. But she didn't intervene the day a reporter asked me how it felt being the top black model in the industry. I corrected him by saying that I was the *top* model, not just the top *black* model.

There would be plenty of backlash from that one comment. Some couldn't believe I would be so bold as to put myself on the same level as superstar white models like Christie Brinkley or Cheryl Tiegs, or worse yet, above them. I wouldn't feel the full consequences of my success, or that bold declaration, until a few weeks later at fashion shoots with other white models. Models who had always been chatty and friendly with me previously now had very little to say. There was resentment and anger toward me where there hadn't been before. One friend suggested I recant my statement. I had no intention of doing that. I had said what I meant, and more important, what I had said was true! Boohoo if it made some people uncomfortable or angry. But I was hurt and surprised by a few of the women's responses to my success. It was just fine if I got a *Glamour* magazine cover here and there, but *Vogue* seemed to be considered above my pay grade. It wasn't as if I'd put myself on the cover of *Vogue*—the powers that be had made that decision.

If that wasn't enough, my own community (i.e., the black community) decided it had issues with me, too. Some were unhappy that I appeared more in mainstream magazines than I did in the handful of black magazines that were on the newsstands, and some even went so far as to suggest that my "European features" were the real reason I landed the cover of *Vogue* and had had so much success in the white fashion world. Funny how my so-called "white features" never helped me get cabs on the streets of New York, or prevented me from being followed by security every time I stepped foot inside expensive Madison Avenue boutiques.

In the midst of all this I got a call from the designer Valentino Garavani, asking me to join him in Italy for a few weeks to serve as his muse while he designed his spring collection for 1975. Valentino was a favorite designer of Jackie Kennedy, and even designed the white dress she wore when she married Onassis. I was happy to agree to the trip.

Those weeks in Italy with Valentino were divine. He spent days draping yards of satin and lace around my frame, and would often ask for my opinion on textures, lengths, and style patterns. Once the day's work was done, I'd spend time lounging around his villa on Lake Como. The designer had an abiding love for Asian culture, and his house featured a massive collection of Chinese figurines.

When I returned to the States from Italy, I began to take acting lessons from the father of method acting, Lee Strasberg. This was the man who trained Paul Newman, Robert De Niro, Al Pacino, and James Dean, among others. Strasberg plays Hyman Roth in *The Godfather Part II*, and his performance in that film sent chills down my spine. That he gave me a positive critique for my acting remains one of the best compliments I've ever received.

As if the year couldn't get any better, in the fall my photographer friend Peter Beard invited me out to his Montauk home to take some test photos for a future layout. Peter was a pretty cool guy who would later marry Cheryl Tiegs, and he was handsome—I enjoyed hanging out with him just for the eye candy alone. He loved all things African and could talk about the motherland seemingly forever. Peter was so good-looking that I question to this day my reason for missing out on that love connection. When I arrived for the weekend at his estate, Candice Bergen was there, too, hiding out from some ex-boyfriend she never wanted to see again. Peter's house was so secluded and secure that no one could find you if they didn't have the exact directions.

As Peter snapped me in different outfits around his large estate, he couldn't stop talking about his latest amazing find in Africa.

This was his usual conversation when we chatted, since he was always off saving some elephant, tiger, or other animal he felt was in danger.

But this time his excitement wasn't about a four-legged animal in jeopardy of immediate extinction. This time he was talking about a flesh-and-blood human, a woman named Iman Mohamed Abdulmajid. Peter kept gushing about how he discovered Iman in the wild bush of Africa, implying, or so I thought, that she had been in some tribal village in the middle of nowhere. He showed me a few pictures of her dressed in traditional African garb and explained his plans to bring her to this country. He thought she'd be a perfect model.

The more women of color in the world of fashion the merrier, so I was happy to give my approval. I didn't give our little chat much thought after that weekend. Just a few months later at a party given at some swanky Manhattan home, I saw Peter arriving just as I was about to leave for the night. On his arm, all the way from Africa, was the stunning Iman. He'd made good on his promise to bring her to the US. Dressed in a gorgeously elaborate African outfit, Iman was far more breathtaking face-to-face than Peter's photographs had revealed. I reached out to shake her hand, and I'll never forget feeling her tremble. She was entering a brand-new world and she was scared to death. Not that I blamed her; I was from upstate New York and felt the same.

But seeing her in person, it was hard not to question the found-her-in-the-bush story Peter had told me, because frankly Iman's skin was far too flawless, her long, slender polished red nails were far too groomed. But my motto remained, "Never knock anyone else's hustle," even though I knew that story would come back to bite someone in the ass.

After Peter introduced us, he asked if I could stay a little longer to get more acquainted with Iman. I was so fascinated by his African queen that I immediately agreed. That was how it all started, the complicated and rather complex sisterhood of sorts that I have shared with Iman for over three decades, and that continues to this day.

I won't lie. My relationship with Iman has been full of ups and downs over the years. I guess this business isn't exactly the best foundation for building trust and lasting ties. At its core, modeling is based on what's on the outside—the superficial—and that can bring a world of insecurities to the surface for women.

But as the years have gone by, our lives have merged and inter-twined in ways neither of us could have ever imagined on that first fateful night at a Manhattan house party.

CHAPTER 10

The Distinguished
Gentleman

There are more than a few advantages that come along with having your face plastered on the front of glossy periodicals several times a year. I would be lying if I didn't admit that one of the biggest and best perks of the bunch is catching the attention of world-famous and globe-trotting wealthy men.

I lost count of the number of times I was invited to dinner parties of rich and fabulous men who only wanted a few hours of my time with no strings attached. One well-known world leader's dinner party came with a stunning Van Cleef & Arpels five-carat ruby ring sitting right alongside the salad plate. I still take that ruby ring out occasionally to admire it and reminisce. But a call in 1975 from one of the most revered men in sports really sent my head reeling.

Arthur Ashe was then, and as far as I'm concerned will always be, the stuff bona fide legends are made of. To this day he remains the only African-American man to win the singles titles in tennis at the US Open, the Australian Open, and Wimbledon. And he was fresh off his win at Wimbledon in 1975 when his agent called and suggested we meet for a cozy dinner date in New York City. Since I had been a serious athlete in high school, I took great interest in the young star's career, and was beyond impressed by his skill, his grace under pressure, and the fact that he'd accomplished so much in a sport that wasn't exactly known for its inclusiveness or its diversity.

The intelligence Arthur displayed during his interviews after his matches was matched by the elegance of his serve. He was a class act, but I thought he was a smart, sweet, and adorable nerd—cute, too, yes, but not someone I would consider dating seriously.

My preference in men had always leaned toward the suave, debonair, and edgy type. I liked men with a certain amount of swagger and bravado. Not a bad boy per se, but not a squeaky-clean guy, either. Arthur was pretty squeaky clean from what I could tell before we met. There was nothing wrong with that, but it just wasn't my cup of tea.

Not that Arthur had much choice in the matter. The world he lived in and the game he played didn't open its doors for just anyone. Swagger of any kind wasn't allowed in the highbrow world of tennis. The fact that he was allowed in at all showed how truly special he was.

I'll never forget explaining my reasoning for turning Arthur down for a date to my guru, James. The look of horror on his face was priceless. Once I'd finished, James took a long, deep breath before explaining the many, many reasons why Arthur Ashe was exactly the man I should be dating at this point in my life. I was one of the most famous black women in the world, he said, and Arthur was one of the most famous black men in the world. That alone should have been enough, but James went on:

"Together, you two are the most powerful black people on the planet. Ponder if you will what you both could do together with your power combined."

James was a cunning mastermind in the way he saw the world and looked ahead to the future. I loved him for that. The symbolism of the combined power that Arthur and I had as celebrities hadn't crossed my mind. We could have been the Jay Z and Beyoncé of the seventies.

James closed his very convincing argument with the sly remark that no client of his would be turning down any offer for a date with Arthur Ashe. By this point, I was in total agreement.

Two days later, Arthur picked me up from my apartment in a black Lincoln Town Car. To my surprise he wasn't nerdy-looking at all. When I sat face-to-face with him, I saw that he was rather noble-looking, with a distinct square jaw, beautiful caramel complexion, and a pair of black horn-rimmed glasses that framed his narrow profile to perfection. He took my hand when I entered the car that night, and the first words out of his mouth continue to bring a smile to my face whenever I think of him:

"I admire the work you've done to get where you are," he said, looking into my eyes. "You've accomplished so much in your career, and I applaud you for that. I admire you very much. Congratulations."

No man had ever given me any kind of kudos in my life, so I was floored by how easy it was for Arthur to express himself so sincerely. In those days, men didn't go around passing out compliments to women for their achievements—or even opening the car door for women for that matter. But Arthur Ashe was a totally different kind of man.

Arthur had been assigned to West Point as a young lieutenant in the army before he broke down barriers in the all-white world of professional tennis. He had also been the captain of the US Davis Cup team and winner of the WCT Finals. The records Arthur Ashe created as the only black man to win those major singles titles remain unmatched and unbroken today, some forty years later. No black man had ever won those three titles before Arthur, and no black man has come remotely close to winning them since.

Now, that's what I call a legend, and that's what I call a hero. So it breaks my heart when I talk to young people today and they say they have never heard of Arthur Ashe. How is that even possible in the age of the Internet?

Arthur's graciousness won me over minute by minute on that first date in 1975. We shared a charming dinner, then went to see a funny movie starring Richard Pryor. Arthur was a bit shy and not the most gregarious man I'd dated, but, hey, I have been known to carry on a conversation for two, so that proved to be no problem at all. He kissed me on the cheek at the end of the night and asked if he could call again. I felt like a schoolgirl after a drive-in movie. Was this my real Prince Charming at long last?

Arthur did call again after that night, and again and again for many nights afterward. I was thrilled. But the nightmare of our busy lives proved challenging for both of us: He played tennis all over the world, and I traveled all over the world for fashion shows and editorial assignments. This was all well before the invention of cell phones, texting, or Skype, so we spoke maybe three or four times a week and saw one another only a few times a month. Still, I found myself falling madly in love with him. And to my surprise, we began to gather our own fan club as news of our relationship leaked out via *Jet* and *Ebony*.

Arthur had taken a good deal of flak before we dated because of his previous girlfriend's race. She was white, and that hadn't gone over very well in either the black or the white community. And since I'd had my own issues with a few in the black community over my infrequent appearances in minority magazines, our relationship was a much-needed boost for both of us in the keeping-it-real department.

Unfortunately, our hectic traveling schedules wouldn't be the only issue that caused friction. Though we had both triumphed over a great deal of racial resistance to reach the top in our respective careers, we were still subjected to endless amounts of discrimination. My way of handling the overt prejudice against my race was to ignore it as best I could and fight off any chance of that poison seeping into my psyche. I couldn't and wouldn't let that happen. To me, that would be the kiss of death, and my parents had always taught me as much.

Arthur, bless his heart, was never quite able to master that much-needed shield of protection. He took every slight, insult, or verbal slur he heard on and off the tennis court to heart. He let the intent of that type of hate hit its bull's-eye—his mind and spirit.

Another problem was that, other than having successful, high-profile, international careers, Arthur and I didn't share very much in common. His childhood didn't come close to the one I'd enjoyed growing up in Buffalo. His mother had died of complications from surgery when Arthur was only six years old, and that traumatic event shaped him in ways I think even Arthur never fully realized.

His handyman father had raised both him and his younger brother, Johnnie, after his mother's death. It had been a particularly strict household. Single fathers during those days were few and far between, but Arthur's was determined to take care of his family with as little outside assistance as possible. When Arthur was growing up, his father forbade him from playing football because of his slender frame. I believe that lay the foundation for Arthur's mild-mannered approach to the outside world. It's understandable that his father wanted to protect his motherless sons from all the ills of life around them—as a parent raising two young black boys alone, he did what he could to guide his children away from danger. Unfortunately, some demons can't be sidestepped or served away.

As the bond between Arthur and me grew tighter, a completely different side of his easygoing and gentle personality came out. I witnessed a part of him that I hadn't been privy to in the early, getting-to-know-you phase of our relationship. As he slowly lowered his guard around me, he revealed a man capable of collapsing into deep and dark moods, especially after long tennis matches, no matter whether there was *W* or *L* at the end. Arthur could slip into a depressed state after a heckling fan called him a name, or another player refused to shake his hand, or a ref failed to call a point in his favor. It didn't take much to send him spiraling down that deep, dark hole for days.

~

Arthur seemed resigned to the fact that, as a black man, he could ill afford to lose his temper in full view of the public. He was convinced that somehow black men who got angry in public wouldn't go down in history as heroes or icons. So he held all the anger and frustration he felt deep inside his spirit and soul.

Arthur once told a reporter from *Sports Illustrated*, "It's an abnormal world I live in. It's like I'm floating down the middle. I'm never quite sure where I am. It does bother me that I'm in this predicament, but I don't dwell on it because I know it will resolve itself."

I didn't love Arthur's mood swings, but I did adore how his brilliant brain worked otherwise. He was a wiz at advising me on my career, and anything else I asked him. And he understood my position as often the only person of color in a room more than anyone else could. He understood perfectly the delicate dance that came from finding ourselves in a world that hadn't prepared for our arrival.

I learned everything I knew through reading books and newspapers, but Arthur's intelligence was natural and instinctive. His brain soaked up information in an instant and stored it like a steel trap. I rarely saw him read a newspaper, but he was as sharp on world issues and events as any expert.

In his downtime, I was his breath of fresh air, or so he often said. He would say that whenever he heard my voice on the phone, he automatically smiled because he knew I'd be able to make him laugh. I certainly did everything within my power to make him smile when we were together. I wracked my brain about how to lighten his mood, how to make him chuckle and forget the concerns of the tour and his game. I just wanted him to put down the weight of the world, which he seemed to carry on his shoulders at all times.

My cheerful disposition, jokes, and the all-night fashion parties I dragged him to whenever he was in New York weren't the only ways I tried to lift my man's lagging spirits. There were also the many passion-filled nights we spent together where I tried to entice him with my womanly charms.

I guess those four-hour, hot-and-heavy tennis matches developed endurance muscles in every area of the body. We had all-night lovemaking sessions, and I'm not exaggerating on the length of time here, either. I was forced to pull out a bigger book of tricks to help him get to the point of no return sooner, or risk some serious health issues of my own. Swinging from the chandelier each and every time we spent the night together was taking its toll on my own well-being. So, one day, I arrived at Arthur's apartment with a seductive cowgirl outfit on.

My top was sheer, my denim skirt was wide, and there was nothing on underneath. I also wore a fabulously constructed cowboy hat to top it off. Thank goodness it worked wonders in soothing and relaxing Arthur enough so he arrived at the finish line just a tad sooner! Success at last!

Once I really got the hang of how to rattle Arthur's cage, he was an amazing lover; he was one of the most passionate and focused lovers I'd ever had, and I kept up my end of the relationship by never allowing a dull moment to creep into our whirlwind romance. I didn't want to take Arthur, or anything about what we had, for granted, particularly given how much time we spent apart. I tried my best to make sure our separations weren't too long, which meant hopping a plane to watch him play as soon as time permitted in my schedule. On one occasion, I was so tired after flying on a red-eye flight that I fell asleep during the game. Arthur called me out about it afterward because television cameras had caught me napping on air. There I was in all my glory, nodding off while Arthur played his heart out. All in the name of love!

A second marriage didn't sound too bad, either. I was ready for another shot at being a wife, and I was enjoying being in a serious relationship with a man who cared about me and really had something going on in his life. But the old folks down south have a saying: "Still waters run deep."

I'll never forget the sound of the phone ringing in my apartment one day as I leisurely reclined on my favorite brown velvet sofa wearing my favorite silk robe.

Yes, Arthur's call had a certain ring that particular day. The ring of doom.

—

Arthur said, "Hi, Beverly, I really need to speak to you."

"OK," I said.

"I've met someone else," said Arthur.

His words hung in the air for a while as I tried to process them. Had the man I thought I was going to marry just said he'd met someone else? What?

"I'm really sorry about this, but it's pretty serious, so I can't see you anymore."

In between all our flights, meetings, parties, two-hour phone calls, cowgirl costumes, and red-eyes, he'd actually met someone else?

Ain't that a bitch? I said to myself.

I didn't use that exact language with him on the phone, though I so wanted to, but I did manage to ask, "What about us?"

He said, "You aren't ready for a serious relationship. You are a party girl."

I wasn't sure what he meant by that, and I didn't really care. He said good-bye and hung up. Sometime later that night, still in a daze, I called him back and asked if we would be going to dinner later while he was in town. I'd lost my mind a bit at that point. He reminded me of our earlier conversation and insisted I not reach out to him again. The cold reality finally hit me, and it hit hard. I had just been dumped by the man I thought would be my second husband, and over the phone to boot.

Who dumps somebody over the phone after a year of dating?

In the end, I cried a bit, mourned a bit, and then realized he'd probably made the right decision. He was truly amazing and one of a kind, but he wasn't for me. Loving him was a full-time job, even a little draining at times, given that he needed a lot of support with the life he was living. I was certain someone else was far better suited to do his cheerleading.

Arthur hadn't just met someone, by the way. He'd met a beautiful and accomplished woman named Jeanne Moutoussamy, a photographer and the daughter of a well-known architect. Her father had designed the building in Chicago that houses *Ebony* and *Jet* magazines, and Arthur met her when she took photos of him for *Ebony* at a New York benefit.

Our paths wouldn't cross again until years later, after he'd had a heart attack in 1979 and undergone two open-heart surgeries. It was suspected that he contracted AIDS as a result of several blood transfusions during the second heart surgery. I was heavily involved in fundraising for a cure for the disease by this time, in light of all the friends I'd lost to it over the years. The fashion industry suffered greatly at the hands of AIDS in the late eighties and early nineties. So many talented and beautiful souls lost their lives: Halston, Suga, Willi Smith, Patrick Kelly, Gia, and countless others.

Arthur dived deep into the fight to raise awareness about AIDS and advocated teaching sex education and safe sex in schools. He worked hard to clear up misconceptions about the HIV virus, such as it only affecting homosexuals and drug users. He so wanted to find a cure and held several fundraisers to help push the research along. He called to ask if I would attend his events, and I happily agreed. I met his beautiful wife, Jeanne, the woman he dumped me for, which confirmed my suspicions that she was indeed the right one for him.

Arthur and I had some wonderful, heartfelt chats, conversations left unfinished from our previous life together. I finally got to see that spark of joy in his being that I hadn't seen before. A sense of passion and drive that had all but eluded him in earlier years was there now on full display. He wasn't in the middle anymore. That was so wonderful to see.

Arthur Ashe died at the age of forty-nine. I didn't attend Arthur's funeral in February 1993, but I was overjoyed with the outpouring of love he received from around the world. He so deserved that recognition and much more. President Bill Clinton posthumously awarded him the Presidential Medal of Freedom for his achievements in tennis, his fight against apartheid, and his fight against AIDS.

At Arthur's request, he was buried beside his mother, Mattie, at the Woodland Cemetery in Richmond, Virginia. Through his wife Jeanne's tireless work to ensure that his unique legacy endures, the Arthur Ashe Stadium now stands as the cornerstone of the US Open Championship in New York, a monument to Arthur's many achievements, reminding the world of the true champion he was and will always be.

CHAPTER 11

What's Love Got to Do with It?

In the wake of Arthur's abrupt exit from my life, I buried myself deep in my work once again. My timing couldn't have been better as Iman was quickly becoming a major force in the fashion world. Her face was now a familiar fixture in print editorials, and she could be seen frequently walking the catwalks of Europe for various couture and high-end designers.

Try as I might, runway modeling and I never really quite clicked. Janice Dickinson, a beautiful, exotic, crazy, fun, and successful model friend of mine, made sure I got booked in a number of European shows, and I did my best to walk the walk of a top model in each one of them. But my best just wasn't good enough on the runway. I never had as much grace as Naomi Sims, or the swagger of Iman, or the perfect hip-to-hip rhythm of Naomi Campbell. In those days, there was no one around with the skill set of the fabulous Miss J from *America's Next Top Model* to help me perfect my stride on the runway.

I was happy for Iman's climb to the top in all areas of the fashion business. Peter Beard regularly asked me for names and numbers of places to get Iman's hair, facials, and nails done, and I happily shared my glam squad. There was no need for shade in a business with so few of us, though I'm not sure many of the other girls (black or white) would have been as kind.

Soon, Iman and I were running into each other more and more at parties, fashion shoots, and dinners, which caused us to form a true sisterhood. Iman seemed to appreciate the fact that she might be in need of more allies in such a cutthroat industry. I'm sure that reality became much clearer after the story Peter had created about Iman being discovered in the great wild bush of Africa was discredited by reporters. (Iman was actually the product of a pretty well-to-do family from Somalia.)

I won't go so as far as to say that Iman and I were the best of friends during our early years in the business, but we were always supportive of one another. I think some people thought we should be joined at the hip because we were the only two black supermodels at the top of the game, but our personalities were very different. Still, we did spend plenty of time together as both of our careers continued to soar. We laughed and cried together—that is, until Iman met a famous, athletic, and very tall man.

Spencer Haywood was a New York Knick and one of the most popular players on the team in the seventies. He and Iman had a whirlwind romance that received a fair amount of press in all the New York tabloids, and they were married a year or so after meeting each other.

For a while I became the dreaded third wheel, tagging along on dates with Spencer and Iman. We were often invited to premieres and concerts, and I couldn't just go alone. After my divorce from Billy, and the heartbreaking split with Arthur, I made the decision to take some well-deserved alone time to figure out what I really wanted and needed in a relationship. Clearly, I wasn't making the best decisions in the romance department.

But sitting in the backseat of Spencer's Rolls-Royce one night after a party and watching him lovingly massage Iman's hand, I was forced to reconsider my self-inflicted sabbatical from love. I was twenty-five years old, the age when most women were getting married, or were already married, or were having children, or at the very least were shacked up with someone. I wanted someone in my life more than anything, but I knew I wasn't going to find it sitting in the backseat of Spencer's big-ass car. I had to get back into the dating world, and fast.

~

For many black women, a trip to a hairstylist is a regular thing. I went every other day—if not every day—to see my beloved James, both for his curls and his counsel. Every now and then James would pull out a list of single men he thought I had to meet. Usually, I listened politely and then quickly dismissed them all with the wave of my hand. I'm not sure anyone understood where I was emotionally at that time. I couldn't rush into yet another attachment. Broken hearts do eventually heal over time, but one never knows how long it will take.

One of James's other favorite clients, Claudia, had a good friend named Danny Sims she wanted me to meet. I knew Claudia well from her weekly hair appointments. Claudia was a well-put-together African-American woman in her mid-forties. She was always tastefully dressed and wore the most beautiful diamond and gold jewelry. I hung out a few times with Claudia and her husband, Tripp, whose real first name I never learned in all the years I knew them. I was fairly certain his mother didn't name him Tripp. Whatever his real name, judging from my visits to their lovely home on the Upper East Side, it was pretty clear they were enjoying the good life. My impression was that Tripp was actually a high-level drug dealer, but no one told me that and I never asked. He was always in possession of large amounts of cocaine and other mood enhancers, which he happily shared, so I assumed that's what he did for a living.

Their friend Danny was a well-known music publisher, and both James and Claudia could not stop talking about how perfect he would be for me as a boyfriend. I realized there would be no peace for me at the salon until I agreed to meet him. I also thought about how Spencer had gently and lovingly caressed Iman's hand that night in his car, and in that instant I gave in. I wanted my Mr. Right right now, so I agreed to meet Danny at Claudia's home the next day. What harm could one blind date cause?

I arrived at Claudia and Tripp's apartment at around seven or so in the evening. We had a few drinks and other substances as we waited for Danny, and boy did he take his own sweet time getting there—he didn't show up until around ten thirty or eleven. Along with his tardiness there were a few other "side-eye" moments that caught me by surprise that night. It was a winter's evening in New York, yet Danny walked in the door all smiles wearing only a pair of khaki shorts and a polo shirt. No coat, no socks, and no scarf. Only God knows why I didn't hightail out of the door without ever looking back.

For one reason or another, neither James nor Claudia had bothered to mention that Danny had a good twenty years on me age-wise, was bald, and was in the process of installing hair plugs! It looked like he had a yard with plots of grass being installed on the top of his head. I wish they'd told me so that I could have avoided my startled reaction when I first saw him.

My dear friends had also withheld from me how Danny liked to ramble on and on about himself. His nonstop chatter didn't allow anyone else a chance to get a word in edgewise, ask a question, or even take a bathroom break. I sat there in the living room with him (Tripp and Claudia had excused themselves for the night pretty quickly) as he talked about himself. I thanked the stars above that I'd had enough mood enhancers that night to block out the vast majority of everything he was saying. We were on the twenty-fourth floor, and I fear that had I been in my right mind I might have walked to an open window and jumped right out of it in order to make him stop talking.

Sensing the end was nowhere near—he seemed to be getting a second wind—I decided to take him into one of the back bedrooms. While I rarely slept with the men I dated on the first night, I made an exception with Danny just in an effort to get him to shut the hell up. He seemed to have fun, and I had several moments of blissful silence. Along with talking too damn much, Danny also had an insatiable appetite for sex that fit the textbook definition of a true-to-life sex addict. Too bad he hadn't mastered the art of it. "Sex addict" wasn't a term fully recognized back in the 1970s, but I certainly learned the meaning of it when I met Danny.

With that good deed done, my hope was that Danny Sims would run along and forget we ever met. No luck there—he insisted on walking me home across Central Park, talking nonstop all the way. I remember slamming my apartment door in his face when we got to my building, praying he'd take the hint that the conversation and date were now really over.

The next morning, I called James to rake him over the coals for his lack of full disclosure about Danny. He appeared oblivious to any of the personality quirks I noticed and attributed them to my disappointments in love.

"You're being too hard on him," James insisted. "You're nitpicking because of your recent history. Don't rush to judge him so quickly."

Per usual, I heeded James's advice. My heart began to really soften as numerous bouquets of exotic flowers began to arrive at my apartment over the next few days. James came over for a peek and just oohed and aahed, though he was less than pleased to learn that I had yet to call Danny to thank him for the flowers. I knew I needed to say thank you—I just wasn't ready for the never-ending conversation that was bound to ensue.

"You're being rude and you know it," James said, as he watered batch after batch of my yellow roses.

What James called my rudeness would be put to the ultimate test when the beautiful flowers morphed into expensive gifts. One day, a gorgeous Mikimoto pearl necklace—the most expensive pearls money can buy—was delivered to my door. It was indeed beautiful, but I felt I would now have no choice but to call Danny and demand that the excessive gift giving come to an end. I mean, I'd met the man one time, and slammed the door in his face at the end of our date. Flowers coming every day were one thing, but a five-thousand-dollar pearl necklace in 1976 was an entirely different story.

Before making that call to Danny, however, I really wanted to know if the pearls were authentic. I guess I needed to see if he was playing games or not, because I wasn't going to thank someone for sending me fake jewelry. If anyone had knowledge about real and faux pearls, it would be my James, the master of all things fine and fabulous, so I dashed over to his salon.

James was with a client when I arrived, but he stopped twirling mid-curl to deal with me. James—who regularly escorted me through Tiffany's massive showroom in an effort to school me on the various types, shapes, and sizes of diamonds—knew all the tricks of the trade as far as jewels were concerned. He did the quick and easy pearl test: putting the pearls in his mouth and rubbing them against his mega-white teeth. Real pearls have a slightly rough texture and faux pearls are smoother. The verdict: My new pearls had a rough texture and were quite real.

With that final confirmation, I decided I had no other choice but to give in, and called ol' chatterbox at his office to thank him profusely for his kindness over the last few days. I also explained to Danny that I could not accept the pearls. He expressed disappointment and then somehow managed to get me to agree to dinner where I could return the pearls in person. How did I ever walk into that trap?

Surprisingly, dinner the next night did reveal a much more fascinating Danny Sims, though his wardrobe remained the same—awful! This forty-plus-year-old man dressed in the way the very wealthy often dressed then—that is, shabbily, to distract people from how much they were worth.

Once I'd gotten over his second horrific outfit of the week, I decided to listen to the words coming out of his mouth in an effort to be as open-minded as James had suggested. Surely a man who talked as much as Danny Sims had to say something worthwhile at least some of the time. Another plus for the man who talked way too much was that, with the exception of Arthur Ashe, Danny was the first black man I'd met who had traveled extensively around the world and had been exposed to many of the cultural experiences I had. In those days, a black man with serious business dealings, international contacts, a hefty bank account, and who didn't play sports or sing songs for a living was a rare find.

So I listened. What I learned was that Danny was the eighth child of twelve, and that his parents had been sharecroppers in Mississippi. He had vivid memories of riding on the back of the watermelon truck as a child while his father tried to sell the melons around town, an experience that convinced him to get as much education as possible. He attended college in Illinois, where he played football, and soon found he had a great head for numbers. Years later, he and his siblings opened a few soul food spots in Chicago, then in Manhattan, and Danny worked in that business until he developed a particular talent for card games.

Danny began setting up card games in the back room of his family's soul food joints using fixed cards that he'd number beforehand and then repackage to look like a new deck. These less-than-honest card games turned into big hits in the black community, and the money began to roll in. But with that kind of cash changing hands, word spread fast, and it wasn't long before the Mob and other organized crime gangs came calling.

In the mid-1960s, Danny headed to Jamaica to meet up with his friend and singer Johnny Nash, who was best known for his hit "I Can See Clearly Now." The two friends formed the record label JAD (Johnny and Danny), and in 1968 Johnny moved to Jamaica to record his own music and learn more about the popular rocksteady sound. There, Johnny met a struggling vocal group with a sound he loved, so he asked Danny to come down to get his advice on signing them to a deal. The group's name was the Wailers, and their lead singer was a dynamic young man named Bob Marley. Danny was sold on the trio from the moment he heard them perform, and all three members—Marley, Peter Tosh, and Bunny Wailer—signed exclusive publishing and recording contracts with the JAD label.

Hearing the story of how Danny had co-discovered Bob Marley and helped bring reggae music to America turned my twenty-five-year-old head completely around. This man was a living, breathing, walking genius. Over the next few weeks, we continued dating, and Danny Sims continued to send even more fabulous gifts to my apartment. One day, shortly after our third date, he sent over a glorious silver fox fur. It was a beautiful piece, but something in me just had to ask for a receipt. My excuse was that I might want to exchange it for a different size or color, but what I really wanted to know was where the coat came from exactly. Had he purchased the coat from Saks, or was it stolen? A girl just needed to know these things.

I didn't ask him this question point-blank, but I should have. Danny must have known that at this level in my career, I couldn't walk around in a stolen coat—I would never live that down in the industry. Danny had perfectly reasonable answers for every concern I presented him with. His furrier had had the silver fox fur specially made for me, and he had his own jeweler, too.

Sometimes Danny would talk about the appeal of open marriages and multiple partners, but would quickly backtrack when he saw my reaction. I loved that he listened to what I had to say on the matter.

Danny had been married twice and had one child per marriage, but I was undeterred by his history, just as I was undeterred that he was an atheist and had diarrhea of the mouth and poor judgment in clothes. I even remained undeterred after mentioning Danny to my ex, Billy, and hearing his negative review of the new man in my life. Billy knew of Danny Sims and his reputation in the music industry, and nothing of what he had heard was very good. But I chalked that up to Billy just playing the jealous ex-husband, so I paid him no mind.

Though I'd met Danny in March of 1976, by April James was already asking if I had given any thought to getting married again. James sincerely wanted nothing but the best for me, and he truly felt Danny could give me that. Danny was already talking to me about marriage, too, so we headed to the diamond district. I chose a not-so-modest five-carat engagement ring that was a little outside the box of what a traditional ring might look like. Then, in some roundabout way, I ended up being the one who asked Danny to marry me! And he said yes.

I called my parents to tell them about my impending marriage, and to let them know that Danny and I would be flying up to Buffalo that weekend for the family to meet him. I braced myself for what was sure to be their anger over his advanced age—he was closer to their age than mine—but lo and behold if Danny Sims didn't charm my parents like he did everyone else. (My parents especially liked him after he told them he would buy them a new house.) Danny Sims was intoxicating, and I wanted to be around him more and more.

My mother suggested we get married in our family's living room on Mother's Day, which we did. A big reason for my parents' acceptance of Danny, I'll always believe, was that he was financially well-off and that he could certainly take care of me for the rest of my life. The tradition of men caring for their wives and families was still a very strong one. Financial security was first and foremost on the minds of my parents for all of their children, and though I had saved most of the money I'd made since my very first modeling jobs, I agreed with them—an extra layer of protection to fall back on never hurt.

The wedding didn't go off without a hitch. As Danny and I readied ourselves to leave the day after our wedding, a sinking feeling came over me. Danny had said his good-byes to my parents and was already sitting in the car that would take us to the airport for our honeymoon in Puerto Rico. But I lingered inside my childhood home, unwilling, or unable, to join him.

My father kept saying, "Beverly, it's time to go."

Suddenly something in me didn't want to go anywhere with Danny Sims. Eventually we went outside, but as we drew closer to the car, my father was now pushing me along, saying, "Beverly, it's time to go to be with your new husband."

By this point, my father had a concerned look on his face, as if it were all sinking in that maybe I should have given my second marriage some extra thought. My family had totally missed the signs of my first marriage being ill-advised.

As my father kept nudging me along, I looked at Danny through the car window and realized he was angry and frustrated. A chill went up my spine when our eyes met, though he quickly replaced that look of anger with a smile as he opened the door for me to get in. Maybe I should have run for the hills, or at the very least run back into my parents' house, where I could have thought things over a bit longer. Instead, I got right into that car and pretended all was well.

I decided to try to enjoy my honeymoon, and managed to do so for about twelve hours. That was around the time I noticed Danny flirting with several women at the bar. So this is what married life to Danny Sims would be like? Confronting him about it later that night in our room proved pointless as he denied any wrongdoing. Then he turned the tables around by accusing me of having issues with jealousy and insecurity. Maybe I was making too much out of things; I didn't want to fight with my new husband.

Back in New York I put my best face forward and moved into Danny's spacious ten-room apartment at Fifth Avenue and 102nd Street in Harlem. Its location factored greatly into why his rent was so low. One of his brothers, Eddie, also lived with him, but I soon realized the hard way that his brother wouldn't be the only one with whom I'd be sharing the apartment. Oftentimes I would return home from modeling assignments only to find many of the artists Danny had signed to his record label sleeping in the guest bedrooms or on the floor of our living room. Old friends of his, former lovers, and goodness knows who else would regularly reside under the same roof with us for weeks at a time. It was not exactly a normal marriage.

One night, after returning from a weeklong modeling job, I found a woman wearing my nightgown running out of my bedroom. She nearly had a stroke when she saw me and immediately started stammering, "Oh, Danny said you wouldn't mind if I put this on!"

"And you were dumb enough to believe that shit?" I said.

Who knows what Danny and his brother Eddie had going on when I wasn't at home. I'm pretty sure drugs of some kind were involved, as cocaine was in constant supply at the apartment courtesy of Danny's many contacts in the music business. My guess was that our earlier talks regarding open marriages, multiple partners, and orgies were coming to fruition behind my back, but I decided denial was a better way to live. I wanted to be happily in love and that's what I was going to be. I knew Danny loved me, despite whatever foolishness he had going on.

Danny began suggesting I study Scientology. I resisted for many reasons. I wasn't all that familiar with Scientology, but I knew it didn't have God in it, and that was really all I needed to know. But while I didn't follow Danny's lead on religion, I did adore his approach to health, cooking, and overall well-being. He was into natural products before they were all the rage. Our apartment was filled with blenders and extractors that he used to whip up celery, carrot, and spinach concoctions of all sorts, which I loved. After years of eating virtually nothing to stay thin, I could now get the nutrients I needed and still stay camera-ready. He even employed a specially trained housekeeper to make the healthy smoothies.

Danny had grand plans for everyone he worked with, and I was no exception. Together, we shared our experiences and our different perspectives and backgrounds to help each other work out how to expand our businesses in whatever way we could. Danny had lots of ideas for me: health and beauty books, major movie roles, and lucrative endorsement deals that would have my face on billboards and all over television. And if anyone could make it happen for me, Danny Sims could.

On the downside, despite all his grand gestures before our marriage that seemed to prove that he had an abundance of money for anything I ever wanted or needed, Danny suddenly became short on cash after we exchanged vows. I was now paying the eight-hundred-dollars-a-month rent on the Fifth Avenue apartment and for recording sessions with upcoming artists on his label. Danny would ramble on and on about waiting for cash to arrive from several of his overseas bank accounts. Sometimes he would say that there had been a mishap with the wire transfers, which meant I had to pay all the bills. I wasn't happy with this, but I had to stay steadfast in my belief that my husband was being truthful with me about his business dealings. I believed he had no reason to mislead me since we were a team.

Our money issues came up in a conversation with my father one night, and I could all but smell the smoke coming out of Tim Johnson's ears over the phone.

"Tell him to go to London and pick up his damn money. He can't keep using yours!"

My father was right—Danny had money somewhere. I knew because he had let me in on the beauty of keeping offshore accounts on the Cayman Islands. But I didn't want to call my husband a bald-faced liar, and I wanted and needed to trust him if our marriage was going to work. If we developed a strong bond together as husband and wife, then surely things would have to get better sooner or later. I was willing to make any compromise I could for him in order for him to see how much our marriage meant to me.

I even made a visit to a Scientology church in Manhattan one afternoon, and spent a few hours listening to all their ideas about life and death. At the end of my visit, the counselors asked for a generous donation, which I gave . . . to the tune of one hundred thousand dollars. The expression on Danny's face the moment I announced my donation was priceless. But not quite as priceless as the phone call he made to the church a few minutes later, demanding they return my check immediately or risk their location becoming a parking lot by the next morning. My check was returned to our apartment within the hour, and Danny never mentioned Scientology again while we were married.

If only every issue in our marriage could have been resolved that easily. Many of Danny's business dealings were troubled, especially regarding his involvement with reggae legend Bob Marley.

Danny had signed Bob and his group, the Wailers, to a less-than-favorable recording and publishing deal back in the sixties, and Bob lost a great deal of money because of it. Though this was standard practice in the music industry, black folks really got salty when black record owners did it to black artists.

The two had parted ways on bad terms in 1972, several years before we married, and they hadn't spoken since. But each time we visited Danny's home in Jamaica, it would have been completely emptied out by looters (even the toilet paper would be gone). We had to replace the furniture and everything inside every time we made the trip down there. People despised Danny in Jamaica because they all believed he had stolen Bob Marley's money. For the most part, they were right.

On one particular visit to Jamaica, we were riding in the back of a cab on the way to Danny's home, when suddenly the cabdriver looked into his mirror and asked, "Are you Danny Sims?"

Danny nodded his head. In a flash, the cabdriver whipped out a shiny, sharp machete from beneath his seat and yelled, "You thieving the music!"

I saw my twenty-five-year-old life flash before my eyes. I would never make it to the age of twenty-six, and I very much wanted to see that birthday. Screaming, Danny and I kicked the back doors open and just about escaped that madman and his machete. Don't mess with Jamaicans and their beloved Bob Marley—they take the reggae icon very seriously, as they should.

Bob was indeed pure light. My buddy Lisa, who knew everyone who was anyone, had introduced me to him at the Roxy nightclub in Los Angeles, years before I met Danny. I then had the pleasure of seeing him several times over the years at concerts and other social events throughout the States and the islands. He was so mild-mannered, sweet, and pleasant to be around. Knowing that I had had such lovely times with Bob over the years, Danny asked if I would call him and arrange a meeting with him to clear the air. It would make a world of difference to Danny's business and professional profile if he could get back into Marley's good graces. Of course I agreed, wanting to do anything to help my husband's business grow, thinking that, when Danny's business grew, we grew. I honestly believed that Danny was on the up-and-up and had Bob's best interests at heart when I agreed to reconnect them. I would have never reached out to Bob if I hadn't believed that.

Being unaware of how deep Danny had dug himself into a hole with Bob, I called the reggae star at his Florida home, hoping to make amends. Bob graciously took my call, and we had a nice chat until the subject of Danny came up. I told Bob that I was now married to Danny Sims, and I can still hear his response in that deep Jamaican accent of his. "I'm sorry to hear dat," he said. "I'm sorry to hear you are mixed up with dat man. He no good for you."

This was hardly the best lead-in for me to suggest a meeting with Danny or to tell Bob that we were coming down to Florida the following week.

I told him that Danny had changed since our marriage. I also told him how upset Danny was about Bob's unhappiness over his perceived mistreatment and financial mismanagement. Marley listened patiently to my defense of my new husband, but he never said yea or nay to an upcoming meeting. That said, he didn't say "don't come" either, and that was a huge plus.

Danny and I arrived in Florida the following week and drove directly to Marley's estate. I told Danny to wait in the car while I searched for Bob in the studio section of his home because I really needed to get Bob in a relaxed state before I mentioned Danny again to him. Bob had the heartiest laugh of anyone, and it didn't take much to make him chuckle. I found him in his studio and we talked about old times. Bob was chilled out, so I asked if Danny could come in and join us. I'll never forget Bob rubbing his freshly done dreads and letting out a long sigh before saying, "OK, my Queen, for you, he can come in." (Bob always called me his Queen.)

I got Danny from the car and excused myself so the men could talk business. After about an hour, Danny and Bob emerged all smiles, as though there had never been a rift between them at all. Danny had worked that good old magic again and now would be managing Bob once more.

I still remember saying a prayer under my breath, "Please don't let me have led the great Bob Marley astray!"

CHAPTER 12

If It Isn't Love?

Despite the misgivings I had about Danny Sims, I was still only twenty-five, and I was certain that I had found the kind of mature love and partnership I'd always hoped to find in a long-term commitment. We'd hit a few bumps in the road during the early weeks of our union, but I was determined not to let them undermine who we were as a couple. We were much stronger than that.

Danny was smart, savvy, and wise in all the ways that counted. From his first two marriages, he knew well what commitment entailed and seemed ready to invest the time and effort needed to make our marriage lasting and meaningful.

I was ready to invest the time, too. Having grown up in a home with parents who had been married for over thirty years, I yearned for that kind of stability. I wanted a love I could always fall back on, with a man who understood me completely, for better or worse, and I was convinced Danny was that man for me. I think it came down to the long talks we had about his life growing up in the South and how he would readily listen to my opinions on whatever topic we

133

discussed. He was old enough to be secure in his masculinity, confident enough to support me in whatever I was involved in, and smart enough to know that two people must work hard in order to build love and trust for a real and lasting marriage.

I hadn't met many men before who understood those relationship principles. Then again, I hadn't met a lot of real men at all. The men I had encountered up to that point were just not mature enough to know what real life and real love actually meant.

Danny understood everything about true love, and wanted a second chance to raise a family. He also wanted to make right what he'd failed at in his earlier relationships. Yet I was still worried that life—real life—was quickly passing me by.

My best friend, Dada, gave birth to her first child at age eighteen, and here I was at twenty-five on my second marriage. But I was confident that Danny was my knight in shining armor, because he was ready, willing, and able to walk with me through the good times and the bad times, because that was what marriage meant to him.

Though we both traveled a great deal for our work, we always made an effort to travel together as much as possible. When we couldn't be together, nothing made me happier than searching for unique trinkets for Danny from the various countries I visited. Danny, too, continued to surprise me with gorgeous jewels whenever the spirit hit him, and our loving bond continued.

As our tie deepened, Danny and I continued our long talks about the dreams I had for my career. Danny was a mastermind of careers, and he enjoyed discussing how I could reach the next level. He saw my future much in the same way I did, growing in multiple directions and existing on several tiers, and hopefully for decades to come. He completely bought into the vision of the movie roles I might get, the cosmetic and beauty lines I could become the face of, and the chart-topping music albums I might record. All this would happen while my face continued to smile brightly from the covers of major global fashion magazines.

I had always loved music while growing up, although I never considered myself a singer in the traditional sense of the word. Danny saw my potential as a singer, though, and he had a laser-sharp eye for identifying talent and a gift for selling that talent to the masses. He was convinced I had a real Tina Turner vibe inside me and that I could have hits because I was such a successful model. So just like that, becoming a singer suddenly rose to the top of my to-do list.

After the *Vogue* cover, I had returned to the Eileen Ford agency because in the end I knew only Eileen could maximize the opportunities coming my way. But one of my new husband's boatload of ideas for my career involved my leaving Eileen Ford once again. Danny wanted me to join the Elite Modeling Agency.

When I learned Johnny Casablancas, the Paris agent, was planning on opening his Elite Model Management stateside, I told Danny that I thought it was a great idea. Eileen Ford had always dominated the modeling industry in the US, and Johnny in Paris. Johnny's move was a significant threat to Eileen, and she knew it. What I *didn't* know at the time was that Danny had gone ahead and devised a plan to get a very handsome paycheck from Johnny Casablancas after arranging my departure and the departure of many other top models who followed my lead. We were established models who loved Johnny's new and fresh approach to the modeling game because he understood better than most that it was a brand-new day in the modeling world, and the old way of thinking just wouldn't do. Johnny also didn't mind letting the wealth trickle down, something Eileen didn't seem to be a fan of. My very presence at the company was crucial in enticing other models to switch over to Elite. And because I had encouraged the other models to leave Ford with me, I believed I would at least receive a small percentage of Elite's annual gross. I would later learn how wrong I was.

Danny also decided he would make himself extra-useful by trying to build my brand in an industry I desperately wanted to infiltrate—the movie business. Robert Evans, the big-time Hollywood studio head who was once married to Ali MacGraw, had always been a huge champion of my acting talents. The two of us had a short but intense love affair in the mid-seventies and had remained friends.

Surprisingly, even with Evans flexing his powerful muscles, I didn't have much luck getting Hollywood to notice me. Over the years, my extensive modeling résumé managed to snag me an audition with Aaron Spelling for the television show *Charlie's Angels*, when Kate Jackson chose not to renew her contract. This was well after Farrah had made her big exit. The role was a huge deal because back then, a black woman getting an ultra-sexy part in a prime-time television show was rare indeed.

Who I am kidding? It's rare today, too.

The only main black female characters on the small screen back then were Florida Evans on *Good Times* and Weezy on *The Jeffersons*. No disrespect to Esther Rolle or Isabel Sanford, the wonderfully talented ladies who starred as those characters, but those two roles didn't exactly scream girl power or sexuality. Instead, they showcased black women in more traditional, nonthreatening, and nonsexual ways, so that mainstream America wouldn't feel uncomfortable.

That was the background to why I jumped at the chance to audition for *Charlie's Angels*. After I nailed my reading in front of mega-producer Spelling and a few others, I was convinced the role was mine for the taking. Three beautiful and strong women navigating a man's world, all the while kicking ass and taking names without a hair out of place? That was *me* all day long. Plus, the addition of a name like mine on a show like that would surely take it back to its Farrah Fawcett glory days! It would be a win-win for everyone.

There was just one problem—my phone never rang. I guess neither ABC nor mainstream America was quite ready to see an African-American woman in such an overtly sexy role on a weekly basis. Or maybe, just maybe, I hadn't nailed the audition the way I thought I had. Race was a serious problem in America then as it is now, but it isn't always the problem every time.

I had been taking acting very seriously, and had been attending weekly classes to sharpen my skills. Still, I'm not suggesting that I was giving Cicely Tyson a run for her money. There were limits to what I could do as an actress, and I knew it. But then again, *Charlie's Angels* wasn't exactly the finest writing television had to offer, either. Still, I spent more than a few nights wondering what if. If I had gotten that part in *Charlie's Angels*, there's no telling where my career might have gone. Farrah did only one season of the show and was the belle of the ball in Hollywood for years.

There were some roles in the movies, too, that I would have loved to make my own. Though a little before my time, *Mahogany*—with its fabulous clothes, well-coiffed dos, and those killer Diana Ross eyelashes—would have been a dream come true for me. And I don't just mean the role. There was also the oh-so-fine Billy Dee Williams as the love interest.

Appearing in *Claudine* would have been a pretty amazing opportunity for me as an actress, too. Diahann Carroll managed to look flawless in every frame, portraying a down-on-her-luck welfare mother. She was initially told by the Hollywood studio behind the film that her regal looks would prevent her from successfully portraying a woman on food stamps, and it's not hard to see why they said that. Diahann is one of the most elegant and refined women in the world, but she is also a first-rate actress, which means she was able to pull off the role so well that she scored an Oscar nomination for Best Actress in 1975. Sadly, though, starring roles like those for women of color were, and are still, few and far between.

So it's little wonder that when I got my hands on a little script with the African name *Ashanti*, I held on tight.

The plot centered on the modern-day slave trade and focused on a white man hell-bent on rescuing his beautiful black wife, a doctor who had been kidnapped by brutal slave traders while on a medical mission in Western Africa. The film was to be shot in exotic places like Israel, Sicily, Kenya, and the Sahara desert. The cast read like a who's who of Hollywood at the time—Michael Caine, Rex Harrison, Peter Ustinov, Omar Sharif, and William Holden would all make appearances in the Warner Bros. film, which practically guaranteed box office success, or so it seemed to me. What more could an aspiring actress ask?

Every black actress in the world auditioned for the part, yet my hopes remained high that somehow I would win the role. The part didn't call for a great actress; the character wouldn't be reciting Shakespeare, and in any case she only garnered a limited amount of screen time.

Again, I was sure I'd nailed the audition. But, again, the only phone call I got was to inform me that the very talented actress Beverly Todd had been given the role. Crushed doesn't begin to describe how let down I felt. Danny came up with a bunch of theories about why I didn't get it, but in the end he had no idea, and he couldn't make it right anyway. There were only a handful of roles for women of color out there and the competition was thick. I just had to suck up the disappointment and move on.

With my dream role out of reach, my heart and mind had to move on to other items on my to-do list. This included making a record and writing a health and beauty book, and having a child. Not that all these things were equal, of course.

Danny would eventually get me a record deal, too, but he was forever putting creative projects together. I once sat in our kitchen and watched him put together an entire Earth, Wind & Fire fifty-city concert tour, with the Emotions as the opening act, all in the course of one afternoon. (During the late seventies and early eighties, those were two of the hottest groups around in R&B.) It was nothing for me to come home and find Donna Summer, Joe Jackson (Michael's father), or Lionel Richie at the kitchen table, talking with Danny about their latest album or single.

Danny began managing the Jacksons, along with Joe, directly as a result of my longtime relationship with the Jackson family. I had met the famous musical group after one of their concerts in the early seventies, back when Michael was still a young boy. The family and I had continued to keep in touch throughout the years, and I even had one or two dates with Jackie Jackson when I visited Los Angeles for work. Michael would routinely dial me up for skin-care tips, too, because he struggled with horrible acne during his teen years. The acne, among other things, scarred him psychologically for the rest of his life. I can only imagine what it felt like for Michael to have grown up an adorable little boy, and then suddenly to be stricken with teen acne, scars that became a magnified horror because they happened in front of the world. I felt so bad for the poor kid, so I would routinely offer him the best tips from the top makeup artists employed by *Vogue* and other high-end magazines on how to camouflage the dark marks left behind from pimples. I also told him to buy a tube of the tried-and-true Black and White bleaching cream to get rid of the dark spots. (This was way before his pigmentation disease, vitiligo, began to take hold of his skin.)

Two years after Michael's death, I was backstage at the close of a concert by his younger sister, Janet, when she told me about some of the conversations she and Michael had shared. He would often tell her stories about our chats, it seems, and all the crazy things we talked about, including the makeup tips. Janet revealing those things about her much-beloved brother really meant a lot to me. Knowing that Michael and his family always embraced and welcomed me into their inner circle made me feel loved and included. It was also nice to get a glimpse into the Jacksons' tight family bond. Despite what's often said by the media about them, they all seemed to be very close, which I loved.

So Danny came through for me in the music world, too, and convinced the best of the best to work on my debut album. Heavyweight producer David Foster was on board to write and produce the album, and Clive Davis agreed to release it on his Buddah Records label. Davis played a pivotal role in the careers of so many music stars, like Aretha Franklin, Barry Manilow, Rod Stewart, and later on, the great Whitney Houston, and he came through for me. Clive and I are still good friends today, and he always invites me to his very chic annual Grammy party. He also enjoys playing the music of his new artists for me from time to time.

After Danny got me the music project, he then moved Betty Wright into our home for several months to get my voice in tip-top singing condition.

Betty Wright was a well-known R&B singer who had gained fame with gritty hits such as "Clean Up Woman" and "Tonight Is the Night." Danny had worked with her for years, and had gone out of his way to make sure Betty got the money she was due over the years for various recordings she'd made. Artists routinely ran into problems receiving royalty payments for music they had written, mostly as the result of poorly written contracts.

I hadn't met many women like Betty Wright before, but I sure loved how she could belt out a song and tell you a my-man-done-me-wrong story like no other. Much in the same vein as Minnie Riperton, Deniece Williams, and Mariah Carey, Betty was also a master at the whistle register—the highest of the human voice—which sent chills up my spine whenever she used it. Danny hoped that with Betty's help I would get somewhere near that register, too. Poor man was living in a fantasy world when it came to my singing talents, but I still was in awe of the way his creative mind worked.

Ms. Betty Wright was full of pure down-home southern charm. She was from Florida and brought all that southern "flava" with her into our house. She also brought along her boyfriend, a Baptist preacher who moved into the apartment right alongside us. Betty and I had our rehearsals every morning using various vocal exercises combined with drinking a variety of exotic warm teas to soothe my developing throat muscles. Given the time Betty spent with me, and the fact that I was never going to win a Grammy award, I had to imagine Betty must have been pretty grateful to Danny for all the back pay he recovered from her record companies.

My husband had two sons from his earlier marriages, two very handsome children he rarely took the time to see or keep in touch with. I pointed this out to him whenever he mentioned the idea of our procreating. My hope was that I could get Danny to understand that this wasn't some game we were playing—if we were going to have children, he was damn sure going to be a real father this time around.

Two of the first calls I made after Danny and I married were to the mothers of his sons. I was young enough to think I could waltz right in and make everything OK between the absentee father and his children. I didn't appreciate the fact that broken families are rarely easily glued back together. One of Danny's boys was in his late teens, and the other was only a few years younger. I insisted Danny get paid up on child support and alimony early in our marriage, too. Then I arranged for both boys to visit their father, whom they had seen maybe four or five times in their entire lives. For me that was unacceptable, not to mention incredibly sad for all concerned.

But by the time bonding with Daddy was over, I regretted ever having the idea of bringing his children to New York. Danny put them to work as soon as they arrived, as if they were his employees and not his flesh and blood. He was not the loving or warm father the boys, or I, yearned for them to have. I'm not sure if it was his sharecropping childhood or what, but Danny seemed ill-equipped to give his sons the love they needed. Maybe Danny hadn't been shown that kind of love as a child. It is nearly impossible to give to someone else what you haven't received yourself. But these were hard-core, real-life realities that I hadn't learned yet.

Despite knowing what I did know about my husband's history as a father, it wasn't long before I had babies on the brain. It didn't hurt that Iman had given birth to a baby girl earlier in the year. I had mostly lost touch with Iman after my marriage to Danny, though she and Spencer did make one visit to our apartment. Nevertheless, I was able to keep tabs on her seemingly blissful union to Spencer and the birth of their daughter through newspapers. She and Spencer still seemed so happy and solidly connected, both mentally and physically.

That's what I wanted with Danny. That's what I always wanted with all the men I loved. Perhaps a baby would give me that peace and contentment I was searching for so desperately and would be just the miracle we needed to make our marriage indestructible. No one could come between us if we had a bouncing bundle of joy, surely. We may have had a shaky start with our rather large age difference and Danny's nonstop talking, but somewhere along the way I'd fallen in love with my balding, shorts-wearing-in-the-wintertime, middle-aged lover. I was pretty sure he'd fallen in love with me, too.

Or, at least, I prayed he had.

CHAPTER 13

The Other Shoe Drops

Infidelity is something no one should be forced to face during the course of a marriage. The fear of being cheated on can drive a woman batty pretty quickly, and cause her self-esteem to plummet, supermodel or not. I should know.

That's not to say that Danny hadn't given me fair warning of what might be coming my way, what with all his casual talk of threesomes and open marriages. But my mind just couldn't fully comprehend the fact that when a man talks of open marriages and orgies, he's really painting you a vivid picture of what your future together might be like.

Danny was a true product of the sixties, where there were few rules about how or where love could or couldn't be expressed. This was a man who would open the front door of our lovely apartment buck naked. Then, he would carry on conversations with our guests as if this were normal behavior. I felt like I spent more time apologizing to visitors than I did actually visiting with them.

Still, I tried to ignore the signs that my husband had possibly taken his attitude of free love and open marriage a step too far by cheating on me. A few months into the marriage, though, Danny wasn't making much of an effort to hide his behavior, and I wasn't making much of an effort to hide my unhappiness.

~

After returning from a modeling trip abroad, I came home to find a mutual friend of ours, Charlene (a sister of one of Danny's brother Eddie's girlfriends), walking out of our master bathroom in a robe. I was already confused to see her come out of my personal bedroom, and then I realized that she was wearing my African silk bathrobe and my Rolex watch. I had bought it on a modeling trip overseas, and had gotten Danny one, too.

It's one thing for a woman you don't know to come into your house and sleep with your man, but it's quite another when you actually know the hussy. What was really bad about the situation was that I'd always liked Charlene. Not anymore. I saw nothing but red, I was so angry. Without a moment's thought, I headed to the kitchen to get the broom so that I could chase after her ass.

Let me stop right here and explain something very important. People often wonder why women go after other women in these situations and not the man. I chose to go after Charlene that day simply because I knew her, and she was in my damn house with my damn Rolex on, wearing my damn silk robe. She had something coming to her, and she got it.

I chose a broom and not a knife because Danny Sims was not worth doing one day of jail time for, but I was determined that Charlene would think damn twice before she brought herself back into my house or my bedroom. She must have seen the I've-just-snapped look flash across my face because she took a running start from the apartment before I could collect my weapon. I was not to be deterred, and caught that heffa downstairs, but she was a quick one and made a mad dash out of the building. I was right behind her though, swatting that broom at her until she suddenly turned into Flo Jo and sprinted down Fifth Avenue.

What a sight we must have been to the doorman, and anyone else just walking by that day! What a blessing there was no TMZ back then.

As I turned to go back inside, I looked up at my apartment and there was Danny, leaning out of the window laughing his behind off. In that moment I realized how absolutely bat-shit crazy my life had become.

My face had graced the cover of so many magazines, and here I was chasing another woman out of my bedroom and down the street with a broom! Could I sink any lower? Actually, yes, I could and I would.

I was in shock. I had to do something to save my marriage. So, in the days following, I reached out to a couple of Danny's best friends to talk some sense into him. I had met them—an older Italian couple (with a daughter around my age)—several times with Danny, and they always seemed to offer him really solid advice, be it about business or life generally, and he would listen. They also seemed to have such a solid marriage, and the husband seemed so dedicated. Maybe Danny could take a few notes.

Immediately after my talk with Danny's friends, I saw a change in him, but it wasn't for the better. He wasn't seeing other women anymore, but now he had turned sullen, despondent, and unpleasant to be around. Our friend Tripp even asked me if I understood what I'd done to Danny by going outside the marriage with our problems. It seems I hadn't made life easier for myself—I had actually made it worse.

Now I really needed a friend.

My first husband, Billy, had warned me about Danny, and I'd refused to listen. Billy hadn't been the best husband, but he had proven to be a wonderful and steadfast friend since our divorce. He would surely understand what I was going through and gladly offer me a shoulder to lean on.

Three years after our divorce, Billy was still the Billy I'd left. He was now living in a boardinghouse in Brooklyn (with a girlfriend who he moved out when I came for my first visit) where he shared a bathroom and shower with a host of other residents. Only now, with a new marriage to another man, could I finally understand and appreciate my first husband. Not everyone is on this earth to become the CEO of a major corporation, or to have millions of dollars in their bank accounts, or to live the high life. Some people are here to offer support and love to others. That was Billy. He didn't need or want constant attention, or his name in the bright lights. I adored him for that, and I just wish I'd had the maturity to appreciate those traits while we were still together.

I guess those were the exact qualities that kept drawing me back to Billy again and again in the years after our marriage ended. I leaned on him heavily during the bad time in my marriage to Danny, though it really wasn't fair to either one of us. I wasn't even turned off by the fact that he lived in a boardinghouse or that I had to sleep in a bunk bed with him.

Those were a blissful two weeks with Billy in his cramped boardinghouse. He wound up offering me much more than comfort, and before I knew it, Billy and I were sleeping together again and I didn't do one thing to stop it. That trip down memory lane would lead to a host of uncomfortable conversations with my second husband just nine months down the road.

After those two weeks with Billy, I headed back home to Danny and realized quickly that I was pregnant. It wasn't the best timing, given my recent weeks away from home, but Danny was overjoyed with my baby news and didn't seem interested in connecting the dots.

I decided I would worry about the Billy factor later and joined Danny in his joy, but neither of us could bask in it for very long. A week after I found out I was expecting, the producers from the film of my dreams, *Ashanti*, called to say Beverly Todd hadn't worked out, and they now wanted me for the lead role after all.

One week I'm chasing a woman down the street with a broom, the next week I'm running away from home into the arms of my first husband. A few weeks after that I find out I'm pregnant, and the following week I find out that I have a starring role in a movie with William Holden and Michael Caine.

Could I really manage a starring role in the movie now that I was pregnant? The film would require me to travel to several locations all over the world and also engage in some pretty physical activity during a few scenes. I would also need to take shots for malaria and yellow fever in order to travel to Africa. Was that even safe for me to do now? Danny thought I could get by, and I wanted the role desperately enough that I convinced myself that it would be all right. The shots I needed were only dangerous to the fetus after three months of pregnancy, and I wasn't that far gone yet. In the end, Danny and I decided we wouldn't tell the director or the producers about my condition. I wasn't showing yet, and we didn't want to give the producers an excuse to say that my pregnancy was a health risk not worth taking.

Within days, Danny and I were off to Israel and meeting with Michael Caine and William Holden over dinner and drinks, or in my case, Shirley Temples. I honestly felt like a little girl whose dearest wish had come true. But as with all dreams, reality sets in sooner or later.

Though the plot of the film centered around Michael Caine's character racing to get his wife (me) back from the slave traders who'd kidnapped her, my character did not appear in all of the scenes. That turned out to be a blessing, given my condition.

By the time Danny and I arrived on location near the Dead Sea on the edge of the Judaean Desert, filming had already begun. I was so thrilled that I had finally landed such a life-changing role that

I didn't even flinch in the sweltering, 110-degree heat. It was still very early in my pregnancy, so I felt extremely well, and looked even better. I shone from the inside out, though I was sure people on the set could easily see the motherly changes in my skin and body. But no one picked up on any clues of my condition until I had a run-in with one ugly, stinking camel.

One scene in the film called for me to ride in a camel caravan to show how I was being transported across the desert in the slave convoy. The scene was slated to last for just a few minutes, and though I hated having to even go near that smelly animal, there was no choice—that was the shot. If I was going to be taken seriously as an actress, I needed to put in the real work, so I couldn't balk at doing unpleasant things. I didn't need any negative reports getting back to the powers that be. Besides, I figured being on the camel for only a few minutes wouldn't be much of a problem for me or the baby as long as I was careful and took my time getting on and off the animal.

Unfortunately, I didn't imagine that my camel would have a mind of his own and wouldn't be cooperating in any way. As soon as I got on, the camel in front of me moved forward as instructed, but the one behind moved before it should have, forcing the camel I was on out of his comfort zone. Before I knew it, I had been thrown off and onto a bed of rocks.

Before I fully realized what was happening, I yelled out, "My baby!" My fall and my cry brought a collective gasp from the crew. My secret was out.

Within an instant of hitting the ground I could feel fluids leaking from my body, and I was in a panic. As the crew lifted me up from the rocks, I looked around for Danny, but he wasn't anywhere to be found. Doctors showed up and examined me and told me that both the baby and I were OK, and that with a few days of rest, all would be well.

Danny, though, was missing in action for most of the day. When I did catch up with him a few hours later, he was in our room with a

young African actress who would later gain fame in a Steven Spiel-
berg movie. Though my darling husband swore up and down nothing was going on between the two of them, for some reason he had
yelled, "It's Beverly," when I opened the door of our spacious hotel
suite. I'm not that big a fool—I know a warning sign for someone
to get dressed quickly when I hear one. (That same young African
lady found her way to New York a few weeks after filming ended—
someone with serious connections helped her get a passport and
other documents with record speed. I would have respected Danny
more if he had tried a little harder to hide his slick ways.)

To be honest, the day of the accident I was too consumed by
my pain and too much in shock from my fall to think much about
Danny's dumb-ass ways. I put what I knew to be true about my
husband out of my head and simply showed him how bruised
my body was from my tumble. And then my dear husband made
what I thought was one of his best suggestions since we had arrived on set—he told me to make a reservation for a massage at
the hotel spa to relax and soothe the muscles of my sore body; he
even suggested which masseur to choose. He was headed back to
New York in any case, so I was going to be alone for the rest of
the shoot.

So having said good-bye to Danny, I made my way down to the
spa and was taken in immediately by the male therapist whom my
husband had suggested. The therapist was a young man, no bigger
than Jiminy Cricket (actually he shared a resemblance to Woody
Allen), and I pointed out to him where I needed him to work his
magic. I would have preferred a woman to work on me, but given
how horrible I felt, Jiminy Cricket himself could have tiptoed on my
back and that would have been pure bliss for me.

I disrobed and climbed up onto the table. While facedown, I
heard "Jiminy" lock the door to the room and then instruct me to
lie on my back. I was bruised both front and back, so I thought
nothing of it until this very small man started massaging my breasts.

I couldn't believe this little hobbit asshole was actually nothing more than a molester. I jumped off the table, grabbed my robe, and stumbled to the front desk to lodge a complaint. One of the women behind the counter quickly whispered to me that others had filed similar complaints against the little twerp.

While I was still at the front desk, the little guy came walking up to me with a huge smirk on his face. Before I could stop myself, I hauled off and slapped the shit out of him and walked away without looking back.

Embarrassed—and not to mention beside myself after a day truly from hell—I headed to my room to call my husband, who by now was on his way back to New York. When I got him on the phone that night to recount the devastating details of my molestation, he began to laugh. My husband actually roared with laughter, as though I had shared with him a joke from Richard Pryor's latest stand-up routine.

And with that, a lightbulb of sorts turned on in my head. That was probably one of the most profoundly revealing moments of my marriage. It was as if God himself were lifting me out of months of darkness and showing me just who the man I'd married really was, once and for all. I'll always believe Danny sent me to that spa for that man to molest me, simply out of pure hatefulness. There was no other explanation. It had been a setup from the start, and I had fallen for it hook, line, and sinker. I had no proof, but nothing else made sense.

I was sure the worst had to be over. Danny was gone, so I would have some peace, for a little while at least. I had no idea how wrong I was. The very next day the police showed up with questions and handcuffs—for me!

"Jiminy Cricket" had filed assault charges against me for slapping him, and now I was in the middle of my own nightmare. I was taken to a courthouse where I was forced to sit on a dirt floor for what seemed like hours. I was desperate to run off my mouth

Emmie Boykins, my maternal grandmother. We kids called her Mother Dear. She had an arranged marriage at thirteen years old.

My parents, Gloria and Tim Johnson, met and lived in Asbury Park, N.J., my dad's birthplace.

My beautiful mother, Gloria Johnson's, high school graduation picture.

The backyard of my Buffalo home. Me at four years old.

Brother Leon, me, and my younger sister Joanne having fun wrestling in our home.

Older sister Sheilah, older brother Leon, Dad, younger sister Joanne, Mom, and me at ten years old. My younger brother Darren wasn't born yet.

I became a Junior Leader at the Humbolt YMCA in Buffalo at eleven years old. I am in the middle of the top row, best friend Dada is to my right, and my sister Joanne is below Dada.

Eighteen years old and on my way in the modeling world, with my proud mom.

My mom and dad; my big sister's wedding picture is to the left and my wedding picture from my first marriage is to the right. (We wore the same dress.)

Me with Beverly Gamble, my
college friend with whom I first
stayed in Brooklyn, N.Y.

Me and my first husband Billy,
December 27, 1972, on a plane to
Barbados for *Glamour* magazine.
Taken by Patrick

Me and my best
friend Dada,
opening presents
with her husband at
their wedding.

Two-day-old Anansa and me in the hospital. The happiest day of my life.

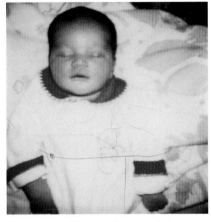

My beautiful angel, Anansa, at one week old.

A happy time at home in 1978, with husband Danny Sims, my mother, and baby Anansa, three days old.

Anansa swimming in the pool at my East Side home in Manhattan.

Taking Anansa to work with me in 1979.
Photographed by Anthony Barboza

Anansa with the haircut
her father gave her.

Anansa and me in South Africa.

Anansa with a puppy, a gift for
her twelfth birthday.

1980s AIDS awareness ad photographed by Gideon Lewin. Me, Janice Dickinson, Bitten Knudsen, Jane Hitchcock, and good friend Rosie Vela.
© Gideon Lewis. Gowns by Joanna Mastroianni

This is the cover! Photographer Francesco Scavullo; Way Bandy, makeup; Suga, hair stylist; Frances Stein, editor.

Cover (with cover lines) of the August 1974 issue of Vogue; *Photo by Francesco Scavullo; Model Beverly Johnson in Kaspar for J.L. Sport sweater with a Ferragamo scarf. Credit: Scavullo/Vogue;* © *Conde Nast*

One of my favorite *Glamour* magazine covers. This is how I saw myself.
Cover (with cover lines) of the July 1972 issue of Glamour; *Photo by Susan Wood; Model Beverly Johnson. Credit: Wood/Glamour; © Conde Nast*

I loved this cover because I could show my hair. I usually wore my hair pulled back for *Glamour*.
Cover (with cover lines) of the December 1976 issue of Glamour; *Photo by John Stember; Model Beverly Johnson. Credit: Stember/Glamour; © Conde Nast*

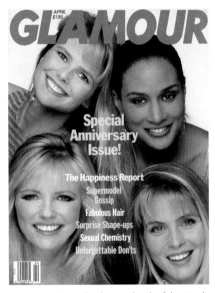

Glamour March cover.
March 1972 cover (with cover lines) of Glamour *magazine; Photo by Mike Reinhardt; Model Beverly Johnson. Credit: Reinhardt/Glamour; © Conde Nast*

Cover (with cover lines) of the April 1989 issue of Glamour; *Photo by Patrick Demarchelier; Celebration of Models. Credit: Demarchelier/Glamour; © Conde Nast*

Beautiful Iman arrives in America.
Photo by Peter Beard

Peter photographs
me in Montauk.
Photo by Peter Beard

Johnny Casablancas Christmas card, 1980, featuring Peggy Dillard, Debbie Dickinson, Andie MacDowell, Sheilah Johnson, me, and Iman, among others. Johnny Casablancas was the founder of Elite Model Management in New York.
Janice Dickinson

Beverly in swimsuit.
Jet magazine

Arthur Ashe, me, Ahmad
Rashad.
Jet *magazine*

Quintin Yearby, my
closest friend, and me
hanging out at a club.

In Scavullo's studio with good friend and hair stylist Harry King and my personal assistant, Jimmy Hester, in the 1980s.

At a Nikki Haskell dinner party in 1990 with actor Chris Noth and Robin Byrd.

Me, my father, and my mother at Benny Medina's home in L.A., 1988.

Dad, sister Sheilah,
Mom, brother Leon,
me, younger brother
Darren, Anansa,
nephew Jason, 1990.

Mike Tyson in my
New York City
apartment with
a friend.

Me with Nikki Haskell, and my date, Benny Medina, at Richard
Perry's home on New Year's Eve, 1988.

Deborah Gregory, creator of the Cheetah Girls, me, and
fourteen-year-old Anansa at a restaurant.

to the police, and let them know exactly who I was and who they were dealing with! Clearly they didn't understand that I was an American, and a well-known one at that. But a voice inside my head told me to keep my mouth shut because I was in a world of trouble thousands of miles away from home, where I didn't speak one word of the language.

After what seemed like a lifetime, Georges-Alain Vuille, the producer of the movie, arrived to post bail (five hundred thousand dollars). Georges was a nice guy—he had a Napoleon complex, but he was a nice guy—and wanted nothing more than to become a big-time Hollywood producer. I could tell by the look on his face that day that my arrest and all the buzz that surrounded it might seriously threaten to put this movie, and his career, in jeopardy. Filming had already been delayed a few weeks when they decided to replace Beverly Todd with me, and Georges could ill afford any more interruptions in the process without causing a considerable backup in the production. And the fact that the police had taken my passport after my arrest meant I wouldn't be able to travel with the cast and crew to the other filming locations. This would ultimately lead to another significant delay for the film.

With all that in mind, Georges understandably asked me to refrain from discussing the incident with anyone and to just finish filming my scenes quietly. My goal was to do as he asked since I really did like Georges and I was so grateful for the incredible opportunity he had given me.

I swear I had every intention of doing what he'd asked, even after Michael Caine made jokes about my great right hook on my first day back on set. But all bets were off when a maid at the hotel suggested I got what I asked for by taking my clothes off in front of a man who wasn't my husband.

Right then and there I knew I had to speak up for myself. That night, I called down to the front desk and requested they gather all the reporters hanging around in the lobby to meet me for a press conference in the morning. Next day, I told my story, describing exactly what had happened on the massage table, and vowing that I would return to Israel for the trial to clear my name and fight for the rights of women for as long as it took.

My heartfelt, though possibly ill-advised, press conference reached all the local papers the next day, and just like that public opinion turned in my favor. Within twenty-four hours the police had returned my passport to me and Georges received all his money back from my bail. The rest of filming proceeded problem free, but the story wasn't over just yet. Drama or no drama, working with the likes of William Holden and Michael Caine was truly one of the high points of my career, particularly since this was one of Holden's last films before his death in 1981.

After I returned home to New York, "Jiminy" found his way to the States and sued both Danny and me for emotional distress. We were advised by our lawyers to pay him off so he would just go away, and we did so. I'll never know if Danny did or didn't plan that horrible event, but if it was a twisted joke on his part, that little masseur certainly got the last laugh.

With that mess finally put to rest, I could focus on the final months of my pregnancy in the comfort of my own home. I was also putting the finishing touches on the record that I had grown more and more excited about while I was away filming. I could really feel the groove of the disco singles I was recording, and could see the songs finding fans in the clubs.

Maybe because he felt some guilt, Danny arranged for me to record the title song on the soundtrack for *Ashanti*, which meant I would have twice as much exposure when the film was released. That also meant twice as much work, which worried my family. My mother wasn't pleased at all with the long hours I was putting into my career with modeling, an album, a movie, and all the other things Danny was adding to my plate, and all with a baby due any day. "He's a modern-day slave driver, if you ask me," my mother would say.

Another new wrinkle in our already-less-than-happy marriage was the arrival of an FBI probe, which Danny assured me meant absolutely nothing. I still remember clearly the first day the feds stopped by our apartment. I nearly lost my mind when I saw them at the door. Why would FBI agents be at our door? Why would they need to come to our home to talk to Danny about anything? He, on the other hand, didn't seem a bit concerned about them nosing around, telling me to invite them in and offer them some coffee or a cool drink. He chatted with the agents for what seemed like hours and never once bothered to tell me what they talked about, which was more than OK with me—I didn't want to know. I had a gnawing feeling in the pit of my stomach that the less I knew about my husband's life, the better. But I would learn the true nature of the FBI agents' visits sooner rather than later.

As my baby's arrival approached, I have to give credit to Danny for helping me adjust to a healthier way of living. He taught me to eat and drink more natural juices and grains for nourishment. On a much less pleasant note, my husband was also obsessed with clean bowels—mine, his, Bob Marley's, and everyone else's. This borderline-sick obsession led him to install a colonic machine in our home. This was a decade or so before most people had come to understand the importance of cleaning out the fecal matter that can accumulate and harden in the colon. My brilliant husband was eons ahead of his time in many ways, but he still had no answer for how to mask the foul odor that flowed constantly through our ten-room apartment as long as that machine was in use.

Funk aside, we also decided on a natural birth without the aid of pain medicine. On the one hand, I did love how much of a health nut Danny was and that he believed so much in natural this and that. On the other hand, he thought nothing of snorting cocaine or indulging in some other harmful drug whenever the feeling hit him. And that was often.

Since I never knew what I was getting with Danny, I finally gathered the nerve from somewhere to tell him that I'd slept with my previous husband nearly nine months before. Translation: This baby could very well be Billy's.

You could never predict what Danny was going to do in any particular situation, and this was another example. Upon hearing my admission, he simply nodded his head and went back to reading his book. (I, on the other hand, breathed a deep sigh of relief.)

About three weeks before the baby was due, I decided to throw myself a yellow-themed baby shower—yellow, since we had no idea if we were having a girl or a boy. I had been so overwhelmed with filming the movie, recording my album, and writing my book that both sisters and my best friend in the world, Dada, had pretty much given up on trying to figure out the best time to give me a shower. So I decided to throw my own!

Ivana Trump gifted me with her fabulous corner suite at the Plaza Hotel overlooking Central Park, and for my special day I wore a delicious indigo-blue pantsuit that accented my golden, motherly glow.

Before all the critics start in on me, let's get this out of the way right now: During the seventies, not all doctors warned you of the dangers of drinking, smoking, or doing drugs during pregnancy as they all do now. So it wasn't uncommon to see women drinking a beer, smoking a cigarette, or smoking a joint while pregnant, and yes, my baby shower had a little bit of all of the above.

My guests had a marvelous time that day, and so did I. I was showered with the most lavish gifts for my baby—I spent the afternoon opening gift boxes filled with cashmere onesies, Gucci infant towels, Missoni baby blankets, Tiffany piggy banks, Cartier sterling silver combs and brushes, fourteen-karat gold rattles, satin baby gowns, and Louis Vuitton diaper bags.

That afternoon was also filled with more valuable tips on motherhood than I was ready or able to take in. Claudia, the woman who introduced me to Danny, gave me the most controversial mothering tip of the afternoon. Honestly, her advice still haunts me. Claudia suggested I join her in the hotel suite's bathroom to do a one and one in the bathroom. She said that would help encourage the baby to make an earlier appearance. My shower was the week before Christmas, and my due date wasn't until January 12. I still had a ways to go, and Claudia—a mother of three—wasn't convinced I could make it without some help. I was huffing and puffing a bit at this point, what with the swollen feet and ankles. Claudia was also more accustomed to seeing me at my comfortable modeling weight of 107 pounds. (I was 163 pounds at this point, and having a tough time moving around.)

Claudia assured me that she had done a one and one before the birth of each of her three children and had experienced absolutely no problems or side effects. I had been around Claudia's kids, and they all seemed perfectly fine to me. So trusting Claudia's motherly wisdom— and my own experience with handling cocaine—I did indeed do a one and one that day in the bathroom of the hotel suite, all while my baby shower was going on outside. And I thought nothing of it.

Looking back after all these years, I thank God each day that my actions didn't cause any harm to my unborn child.

Just as Claudia predicted, a few days later, on Christmas Day, my contractions began. I was in so much pain that I called my mother for advice on what to do because my mind just drew a blank. She told me to get my husband to take me to the hospital immediately. Danny seemed less than convinced it was time for the baby's arrival, and proved it by refusing to allow our doorman to secure a cab for us. Instead, he decided we should walk to the hospital even though it was freezing outside. Mount Sinai Hospital was six or seven blocks from where we lived, and the silver fur coat I wore could barely cover my huge stomach.

Danny, who was well over six feet, walked very fast and left me in the dust. I tried to keep pace as the wind blew me back and forth. For six blocks he never once looked back to see if I was keeping up or had just plain fainted in the street from the sidesplitting pain. As we walked, I remember imagining all the ways one could kill a husband and dispose of his body where no one could find him. That's what walking for blocks on end in the freezing cold while going into labor can do to your mind.

When we arrived at Mount Sinai, the doctors decided my labor wasn't far enough along and sent us back home. The next day I was in agony again, and this time my mother instructed me to return to the hospital and demand to be admitted. And once again, my husband insisted on repeating the same routine. No cab—we walked the six blocks again to the hospital with Danny walking ahead of me while I struggled to fight the brutal wind whipping across my face as I wobbled down the street.

This time, I found some peace and comfort at the hospital after finally being admitted. I'd been suffering from crazy pain after a two-day labor, so my ob-gyn came in and announced that he would be administering an epidural. Danny hit the roof. It was a good thing we were in the hospital because I was convinced he was about to have a stroke as he began to rant and rave about our decision not to use painkillers and how important it was we stick to that plan.

As for me, I'd let go of the notion of a drug-free birth by the first contraction. My doctor and I were clearly on the same page, and he could sense the tremendous amount of stress and strain I was under. As Danny continued to rant, my doctor calmly told him that his presence was no longer necessary and sent Danny home to wait for a call about when he should return. Danny was dumbfounded, and for once had no response. He eventually asked the doctor if he could at least remain in the hallway outside my door, to which my doctor replied, "No!" My doctor was quite "gangsta," and I loved him for it. He wanted Danny out of the hospital, and he wanted me to have peace.

And with that, Danny, dejected, turned around and left my hospital room without a word.

Danny arrived back in time for the debut of Anansa Sims, named after my character in *Ashanti*, on December 27, 1978, at 5:00 a.m. While I know most mothers feel that any one of their offspring is the most gorgeous, perfect, and amazingly beautiful child in the world, my baby girl actually was.

Anansa was the most beautiful and angelic infant I had ever laid eyes on, and I was floating on a cloud from the moment she was born. Danny took her right out of the doctor's hands the second she showed up and held her so long that the doctor had to say to him, "I think the mother should hold her baby now, don't you?"

My doctor really didn't like my husband.

~

The month that followed Anansa's birth was without a doubt the happiest and most magical of my life and of my marriage to Danny. Holding that sweet little baby girl in my arms was such sheer joy every day. I'm not sure if I'd ever imagined the elation and delight that would come with the birth of a child. The feeling I got from just watching her sleep, or coo, or smile back at me, is still so hard to put into words. Danny was on top of the world right along with me, and stayed in the kitchen cooking meals and mixing up all kinds of concoctions for me to drink. Our house belonged to just the three of us those four weeks as people gave us space and time to bond with our beautiful new angel. If I could have scooped up and saved that magical time in a bottle I certainly would have. Life wouldn't get any better than it was during that little slice of heaven back in late 1978 and early 1979.

CHAPTER 14

Bob Marley, the Devil, and Me

Home life with my baby girl was so wonderful that I could imagine retiring from the modeling game at the ripe old age of twenty-seven. I had never dreamed of such a thing before Anansa came into my world. That month away from work was the first time I ever had four weeks completely free since I was a teenager working at the YMCA in Buffalo.

The fire, passion, and trust in my marriage with Danny had been rekindled by the arrival of our little ladybug. For a time, all seemed right with the world, with our world.

But there were still flashbacks to days gone by, though I tried to dismiss them as figments of my imagination. For instance, Danny suggested we hire that African actress from the set of *Ashanti* as our babysitter, and I later found the beads from her braids under our bed. When I asked him about the beads, he told me that she had lost a few of them while searching under our bed for the baby's bottle or while searching for an extra diaper. No way she lost those beads while actually being in the bed with him. "How silly it was to even think such a thing," was his response to me when I asked if he were up to his old tricks.

His flimsy denials kept the family afloat for a while, but soon other issues would derail my happily-ever-after-ever scenario.

Promotion of my movie, *Ashanti*, was set to go into high gear near the end of January 1979. As a part of my contract with Warner Bros., I had agreed to spend six weeks traveling around the world doing press junkets and interviews. But when I signed that contract, I'd had no idea the press tour would come right on the heels of the birth of my first child. And I honestly believed that after Anansa was born, Danny would work his mojo behind the scenes to get me out of my agreement in light of our special circumstances, or at least get it down to three weeks from six. Did the movie studio really expect me to leave my newborn in the middle of breast-feeding to fulfill that kind of a demanding schedule? Could they be that heartless? Apparently they could.

So I was off, away from New York, my husband, and my sweet baby girl.

Fortunately, my darling Mother Dear, my maternal grandmother, agreed to move into our apartment to take care of my little angel, which was the only way I got a little bit of peace of mind as I boarded a plane to travel to the other side of the world. She was the kindest woman I've ever known, and I knew she would give the same love and care to my baby that I would.

As hard as it was being so far from home, I did my best to don a happy face as we traveled across Europe. But feelings of gloom and doom became too difficult to mask after the first two weeks or so. Postpartum depression wasn't recognized as a debilitating condition at all in those days. I cried all the time and I had no idea what I was feeling or what to do about it, either. Being so far away from my month-old baby was just unbearable, and my heart ached for her.

On my nightly calls back home to New York, my sweet Mother Dear would put the phone near Anansa's mouth so I could hear her breathing and making those adorable cooing sounds. Once those phone calls ended, I would roll my body into a tight ball on the hotel bed and cry myself to sleep.

Despite those torturous six weeks on the road doing press, the movie ended up flopping at the box office in the US anyway. All my traveling had meant pretty much nothing at all. Even worse, by the time that press tour ended, the quiet life I'd fallen asleep dreaming about so many nights while abroad had become nothing more than a nightmare. Instead of just the three of us, my home was once again filled to the brim with nameless people from the music industry, all looking for a place to lay their heads for the night—or several nights. My husband was more than happy to oblige them as always.

What was worse, Danny's partying ways had stressed Mother Dear out so much that she'd ended up in the hospital. When I went to visit her the day after I got back to New York, she told me point-blank, "You have to leave that man. You can't stay with him." I could tell my grandmother had been through an ordeal so I didn't raise her blood pressure any higher by asking a host of questions.

Danny was dancing with the devil, and enjoying every moment of it. The new father of a two-month-old baby girl saw absolutely nothing wrong with having endless numbers of strange people streaming in and out of our home at all hours. People were smoking, drinking, participating in orgies, or inhaling endless narcotics, all while our daughter slept in the next room. One night I raced down the hall from my bedroom to Danny's office with Anansa wrapped tightly in my arms. I was pissed about a particularly loud voice and loud music that had been booming in the house for hours. I had a colicky baby who needed to sleep and I had an 8:00 a.m. photo shoot the next morning. (Somebody in the house needed to go to work.)

When I went to ask Danny to keep it down, I noticed that R&B

singer Teddy Pendergrass was in the corner of the room. Now it all made sense—it had been Teddy's big and booming voice spreading throughout the apartment all night.

I remembered Teddy well from his days as the lead singer of Harold Melvin & the Blue Notes. By 1977, he was at the top of his game, starring in his infamous women-only concerts. At those sold-out shows, Pendergrass would belt out his top-selling tunes— "Turn Off the Lights" and "Close the Door"—to a sea of swooning women. My girlfriends and I agreed—Teddy was the man.

I loved Teddy's music, but I certainly wasn't happy with Teddy that night, and as if he could read my mind, the gorgeous soul singer moved toward me, took my hand, and apologized for all the noise he'd made. Then he complimented me on having such a beautiful baby. He also promised I wouldn't hear another peep from him that night. Teddy began sending me a dozen red roses on my birthday after that night, and did so every year until his death in 2010. What a class act and a beautiful man.

The same couldn't be said of the man I married. The fabric of our union was beginning to unravel. The closeness I had felt with Danny just a few months before, after Anansa's birth, had now been replaced by varying degrees of disdain and anger. I couldn't believe the blatant disregard he had for me and for the health and welfare of our baby.

What a difference a year can make. I'd grown up a lot in the months since I'd gotten married, and now I was finally seeing clearly. It wasn't a very pretty picture, and making matters worse I had absolutely no idea what I was going to do about it. For better or worse, I loved Danny very much, and he was Anansa's father. Goodness knows I didn't want to walk away from yet another marriage, feeling as if I had failed again. But I didn't want to be miserable, either.

I went back to my old ways of dealing with the unhappiness and resumed my extended trips away from our home. This time, I had my baby girl in tow, so we could both escape the madness of Danny and whatever he was going through. But this time, I also knew much better than to head in Billy's direction again. Danny never mentioned the possibility of Anansa being Billy's child, and I certainly never felt the need to bring the topic back up. When I was back home, on the days I got the nerve to leave the apartment, Anansa and I would spend time with my sister at her home in New Jersey, or with my parents in Buffalo, or with James in New York. Anansa and I would stay for a day, or sometimes two or three, with friends and family—just enough time for us both to relax. My stomach was beginning to hurt all the time, but I tried to ignore it. I traveled a great deal for my work and barely had time for visits to the doctor. With a new baby and a bad marriage, I had little time to focus on anything else, and that included my health.

Compounding matters was my growing guilt over what I knew was happening to my beloved Bob Marley.

Bobby was now coming around the apartment on Fifth Avenue more regularly as he and Danny were working together again on new music and additional tours. I'd made the call that brought Danny back into Bob's life, and boy, was I kicking myself all the way down the block for that. In truth, I hadn't known Danny but a few months when I made that call, so I'd really had no idea what I was talking about. I had no business getting those two back together, and Danny had no business asking me to.

Bob had told me that I should be wary of Danny, and instead it was I who changed his mind. Deep down, I suspected then that Bob knew better; he had to after all he'd been through with Danny in the past. But still he listened to me. What a mistake for both of us.

~

Bobby was a man with a heart of pure gold. He gave everyone the benefit of the doubt, until they gave him reason to think otherwise, and he wasn't prone to think ill of someone for no reason.

He was also physically perfect. That ruddy red complexion, those glistening, beautiful dreads, and that toned, compact body. Bob Marley was such a good-looking, tidy package. I'll admit I was quite smitten from the second I heard that sexy Jamaican accent, too. He asked me for a date once, and I probably would have accepted his request if he hadn't had a wife. In fact, I think he had several wives, and many, many, many children, on top of that, all of which was a deal breaker for me.

But I always kept love in my heart for Bob Marley, so the thought of putting him in jeopardy the second time around with someone who meant him harm really upset me. It's one thing to hurt yourself by getting into a bad situation, but it's quite something else to drag someone along with you into a mess.

When I think back, there were many indications not only that Bob's reconnecting with Danny was a mistake but that Bob's health was also beginning to fail. Danny often offered Bob a boatload of concoctions for a vast variety of ailments whenever Bob came over to the apartment. I never gave much thought to it and just figured it was nothing very serious. Bob was only in his early thirties, and he seemed to be enjoying his ever-growing fame and riches.

By 1975, the entire world knew who Bob Marley was, and Danny played a huge part in helping him get the recognition he deserved. But Danny probably also took more than his fare share of the profits from Bob's success the second time around, just like he did the first time.

Bob often complained of pain in his foot and in his big toe, but I was honestly so consumed by my own domestic issues that I could barely take time to ask him for more details about his health. Sadly, as it turned out Bob was very ill, and I will always believe his illness was compounded by Danny's unsavory business practices. Bob had given Danny way too much power over his career again, with the hopes that Danny would take him to an even higher level of stardom. Danny did just that with Bob's career-defining album *Exodus*, the one that featured one of Bob's most beloved songs, "Jamming." But Bob was an artist through and through; he didn't have a head for business, he just wanted to make good music. It was a shame that he didn't have his own lawyers to prevent Danny from doing exactly what he had done before. Danny attached his name to the publishing of Bob's music and in the end received huge profits on the back of Bob's songs. I'm not sure when Bob found out he was probably being mismanaged again, but when he realized that his family might not reap the full financial benefits of his work, it must have been a hard pill to swallow.

Danny also advised Bob about his health issues. He and others told Bob not to have his entire toe amputated after doctors found a form of malignant melanoma under its nail bed. Several doctors had suggested removing the entire toe to prevent the cancer from spreading elsewhere, but instead, Bob just had the nail and the nail bed removed, and continued to work and tour to make money.

As horrible as this may sound, looking back I feel certain that Danny knew Bob and his music would be worth far more in death than in life. How else could you convince a man so young and full of vigor to forgo a life-saving medical treatment for such a serious disease? Yes, Bob was a Rasta, and Rastafarianism has certain beliefs that lean toward a more natural approach to life. But I don't believe for a minute Bob knew he was signing his own death certificate by not using traditional medicine. It took three years for the cancer to spread to Bob's lungs, and ultimately all the way to his brain, before stealing him away in 1981 at age thirty-six.

I cried the entire day when I heard the news that Bob had died.

After Bob's death, Danny added paranoia to his list of behaviors. As much as I tried to stay away from learning what actually went on in Danny's business, it was hard to not hear disturbing tidbits here, there, and everywhere while at home, since that's where he did many of his business dealings. As just one example, sometimes I heard about the radio station DJs who had to be dealt with for not rotating certain records enough times on air (as they had been paid a handsome price to do). Other business dealings that he was involved in hadn't gone smoothly, and now more than ever the stress was weighing heavily on Danny.

As a consequence of all the stress, Danny was consuming more and more cocaine—it definitely altered his personality, and it scared me to death. I could tell Danny felt something heavy coming down on him soon, and that meant my daughter and I were both in harm's way. I had to make a move.

At this point, I didn't know if the feds or the Mob or both were on Danny's tail. Before our marriage, Billy and others had bombarded me with stories about the Mob helping Danny finance many of his early projects, like the soul food eateries in New York and Chicago. That money also aided him in going to Jamaica to listen to Bob Marley perform, and to bring back to the States the first recordings of reggae music.

Now it seemed all those old debts were coming due faster than Danny could handle them. I didn't see how he could ever have *hoped* to pay back the money, as he certainly had a habit of spending most of *my* money as soon as I earned it. As his erratic behavior deepened, I tried to make myself more scarce around the apartment.

But sometimes I'd get so fed up with his foolishness I just couldn't help confronting him. After a trip to the bank one morning, I realized my money was disappearing at warp speed. I was tired of Danny's myriad excuses for why my money had to be used for every expense we had. He was in the bathroom washing his face, and I stood at the door and asked him about the money situation in the calmest voice I could muster.

But it didn't matter how calm I was—Danny didn't want to hear my complaints about our finances. Before I really knew what had happened, Danny had slapped me across the face. It wasn't hard—in fact it shocked me more than hurt me—but he hit me, and that was enough. I went into Anansa's room—she was about six months old at this point—and sat in the chair by her bed, just staring into space for a while. What was I going to do now? My husband was spending my money, and now he was raising his hand to me. My Mother Dear was right—I couldn't stay with this man.

Looking back, I see that there were many bad moves I wish I could take back, and the one involving James tops the list. I had to do a modeling assignment for the Neiman Marcus catalogue in New Jersey that next day, so I packed up and took Anansa to James's apartment. I had only planned to be gone for a few days, to clear my head. Catalogue modeling was a quick way of making good money, and by the way the wind was blowing, I knew I would soon be in great need of some extra cash.

That trip to James's house would turn out to be our last time together.

When I arrived back later that night after my day in New Jersey, I found all types of commotion outside of his apartment complex. The doorman told me that James had been robbed, and that both he and my baby were gone. I knew straightaway that the robbery was connected to Danny somehow, so I rushed home to see if he had taken back Anansa. When I got home, sure enough there was Anansa.

When I asked Danny what had happened, he simply said, "That will teach you to run off with my baby."

I started to call James over and over to see how he was, but he never answered. Now I was getting very worried. What had Danny done to my friend? Later on that night in the kitchen, I saw what looked like a man's diamond tennis bracelet broken into pieces. It looked identical to the one James had worn for years. As I stared at the shattered jewelry, one of Danny's friends walked in and began telling the story of what had happened. He explained how James had been roughed up; the bracelet had been cut off his arm, and he had been tied up with garbage bag ties. Then they had gotten Anansa and brought her back home to Danny.

I was in disbelief as I listened to the horrific story of what they had done to my dearest friend. Where was he now? Was he scared to death? I called James again and again that night and for many nights afterward, but he never answered. In fact, I never again spoke to James, my guru of all things fabulous and beautiful. He moved out of his apartment building a few weeks later and closed his state-of-the-art salon not long after that. Mutual friends assured me that James was indeed alive and well, so I was left to assume that he didn't want to speak to me again. I couldn't blame him really.

There was such a huge void in my world after James walked out of my life. He had been there for so long and taught me so much about everything. How would I bounce back from losing such a valuable and beloved friend? How could I bounce back from knowing the reason for losing such a friend?

The first thing I did after learning what Danny had done to James was take Anansa to live with my sister Sheilah for a few weeks.

—

Life is all about the decisions we make and when we make them.

I needed to decide when to make my grand exit from my marriage because I now feared for my life. Not long after we arrived at my sister's house, she asked me a pivotal question about my husband, or rather about my leaving my husband. Did I think my life was in danger if I stayed with Danny? I told her I did, and without hesitation Sheilah said, "Then you must leave now."

With that piece of advice from my big sister, I headed back to the Fifth Avenue apartment to pack my and Anansa's belongings. It was time to leave that life behind for good, and I felt I needed to explain to Danny why.

If I had been completely on my game that day, I would have turned around as soon as I realized there was no one but Danny in the apartment when I arrived—no maids, no nannies, no hangers-on, no friends. Danny hated being alone, so the fact that he was there by himself should have been a surefire signal for me to turn around pronto and run for my life. But I didn't. Instead, I walked right straight into hell.

I was in the bedroom packing my things when he came into the room, and I knew in an instant I was in big trouble. His eyes were bloodshot, he was high as a kite, and I could tell he hadn't slept in days. I took a running start for the dining room to hide beneath the table, but Danny dragged me out by my legs. In my mind, I knew this had to be it, he was going to kill me.

It was then that he began to yell that I had gone to the FBI and ratted him out.

"To tell them what, Danny? I don't know anything!" I said.

This was true. I didn't know anything at all about anything Danny did—what he was doing or what he had done—and I didn't want to know. I just wanted out.

But Danny chose not to hear me. Though I'd broken loose from his grip, he began to chase me around the house, tearing at my clothes and punching me in my face. I could feel my lip bleeding, and then, all of a sudden, he just stopped talking. He told me to be quiet and still. Then he looked at me and said, "Did you hear that? They're coming."

I'm thinking, This man is really bat-shit crazy!

Suddenly, he ran off into another room and came back with a big shiny gun, and forced me to get under the dining room table with him because "they're coming." When we were under the table, he told me that the Mob had a hit on him—he was clearly in the middle of some type of cocaine-induced paranoid delusion.

I tried to defuse the situation and calm him down by telling him I would go out into the hallway to see if anyone was there. There were three entrances to our apartment. I walked around and checked all three doors for Danny's sake. I knew by this time that my face that paid all the bills was completely swollen and so was my lip, and I knew I had to get away from that crazy man with the gun. Eventually I was able to convince Danny to come out from underneath the table and to put down the gun.

After Danny finally fell asleep that night, I called my sister Sheilah to tell her the crazy story of my day. My parents were there and heard the entire story, too, and were deeply unhappy with the escalation of physical abuse. Still, I felt compelled to stay there to make sure Danny didn't come after me later, as well as to complete what I came to do in the first place. I was determined to have an adult conversation with my husband about the end of our marriage. We needed to hammer out the basics of the separation, talk about the fact that I would get the baby, and how we would split everything we had accumulated together down the middle.

Later that night I woke up with unbearable stomach pains—I was vomiting and had developed nonstop diarrhea. Danny took me to the hospital down the street, this time in a cab. There, they determined I had colitis. There are various treatments for colitis, but none worked overnight. We left the hospital and went back home, where I was hoping to rest. Before I could get into the bed, my father and Sheilah's husband, Bobby, showed up, and it wasn't for a friendly visit. As soon as Danny opened the front door, my father decked him so hard he hit the floor.

My father was followed by my brother-in-law, who came into the house toting a shotgun under his coat like he was in *The Untouchables*. It would have been funny if it hadn't been so serious. Bobby was waving the gun in Danny's face and shouting at him that if he ever put his hands on me again it would be the last time. My father was in the background, yelling the same thing. Danny swore he would never hit me again, and that we would be able to work everything out as a couple.

Satisfied they had made their point to Danny, my father and Bobby left so I could get some rest.

But I wouldn't be getting any rest that night. Just after midnight my stomach pains returned with a vengeance. Danny gave me a few more pain pills and promised to take me to the hospital in the morning. But when morning arrived, I woke up to find myself in the back of a car, behind Danny and his friend Milton, who was driving. I was barely conscious, but I could see the tops of trees whipping by at rapid speed. We were in the country it seemed, but I didn't know why.

The next time I woke up, I felt like I had been asleep forever. I found myself in a small, stark, white room. The only windows I could see were high up, and they had bars on them.

My crazy-ass husband had gone and put me in the damn crazy house.

CHAPTER 15

Doing Bad All by Myself

It was true—Danny had signed me into a psychiatric hospital on Staten Island for observation. The doctors had heavily medicated me with some type of hard-core sedative; I'd been out for days.

When my head cleared, I tried to explain to the doctors that my presence in the hospital was merely payback from my husband for planning to divorce him and taking our infant daughter away. But the male doctors weren't moved in the least by my story. Judging by the looks on their faces, my tale was one they had heard many, many times before. It didn't help that no one recognized me. Sitting in my room with the walls closing in, I could only imagine what my family was thinking—they hadn't heard from me in days. I imagined that Danny had made up an elaborate story, perhaps that I was out of town on location or on assignment or something else.

I had to do something. There were two young female nurses working in the hospital, and hoping to gain their sympathy I told them what had happened. Fortunately, they believed me—in fact, all three of us were *boo-hooing* by the time I'd finished my sorry tale. The nurses agreed to drive me back to my apartment to get my clothes and my baby. As we were leaving, we passed one of the male doctors I'd spoken to earlier, and I quickly hid my face in case he tried to stop me from leaving. Instead, he smugly said, "You could have signed yourself out at any time you know."

Jackass! Why hadn't I been informed of that before?

The nurses drove me home, and I thanked them warmly and bid them good-bye.

In the apartment, I couldn't believe my eyes—Danny was in the living room watching some stupid movie as though nothing had happened. Fortunately, I could hear that we weren't alone in the house, so I felt safe enough. Danny didn't seem surprised to see me; instead, he actually waved to me, as though I had just gone out to the store to pick up something.

"Hi, Beverly," he said. "I finally hired that Swedish nanny I told you about."

I held my breath and prayed to the good Lord for strength since I didn't want to end up in Bellevue, where they take the real nut cases, or Rikers, where they take the real murderers.

I asked him where my baby girl was since he clearly had gone to get Anansa from my sister's house.

"With the nanny of course," Danny said.

I left him watching his movie and walked into the kitchen. There, a young blond woman was warming baby bottles in a pot on the stove.

I said, "Where's my baby?"

The nanny said that Anansa was in the tub having a bath—my six-month-old baby alone in a bathtub. What was she thinking? That was plain child abuse. I wanted to choke this woman and my crazy-ass husband at the same time. But since I had just checked out of a psychiatric hospital, I didn't want to be taken right back.

With that in mind, I took a deep breath and went to the bathroom, where, sure enough, I found Anansa alone in the tub. I scooped her up and took her to pack our clothes. When we were done, I walked past Danny without saying a word. I would let my lawyers do the talking from now on.

⌒

For the first few weeks after I moved out of that apartment, I stayed with Sheilah and her family. I needed to make sense of my life and map out some sort of plan of what to do next. The first rule of thumb for any woman who is filing for divorce is to get her financial house in order. But what I quickly realized when I started the process of doing so was that I didn't have a financial house to get in order.

When I married Danny, just eighteen months before, I had more than a million dollars in several bank accounts. I'd worked for more than six years and was one of the world's most recognized models. I had barely had any time off since I turned nineteen years old, and had saved almost every dime. I'm a very frugal soul, and after sending money to my parents, I tucked away nearly every dollar I ever made from every modeling job I had done. But I was in for a shock: When I filed for divorce in early 1981, I had absolutely nothing but the photos I posed for to remind me of the career I worked so hard to build. The money was gone.

Making matters worse, the FBI had contacted my lawyers and asked that I come in to meet with them and discuss a case that involved Danny. Though I had kept my first husband Billy at arm's length since Anansa was born, I knew I needed his counsel now more than ever. He had real street smarts and knew exactly how the feds and other authorities worked.

I had lawyers to lead me through how to handle the feds legally, but the legal advisors liked to keep stuff close to their chests. Billy knew the real truth, and I needed to see the entire picture of what I was facing. I had no idea what Danny was involved with, nor did I know whether or not it would lead him to wanting to come after

173

me again. It was just a few weeks earlier that he had come after me because he believed I had ratted him out to the FBI, so clearly there was more to the story of Danny Sims. I just didn't know what it was.

Billy was blunt with me. He told me to say that I was clueless about Danny's affairs in every possible way and under all circumstances. He didn't care if they asked the basics of how he buttered his bread in the morning; I was to say I had no idea. Both of us thought that the FBI was investigating Danny for his involvement with the Mob. I was beginning to connect the dots, and they pointed to that lovely Italian family Danny was so close to, and to whom I had gone for marriage advice. They were his backers, they floated him money, and they had supplied him with all types of products for him to distribute. They were the Mob.

My mind ranged over all the other strange incidents that had happened during our marriage, and there were plenty. It had always bothered me that all the beautiful jewelry Danny gave me would suddenly disappear. He would give me the most gorgeous pearls and glistening diamond rings, only to say he needed to take them out for cleaning a few months later. When he returned them to me, they wouldn't look quite the same. The diamonds were cloudier than before, and the pearls lacked sheen. Too green to understand exactly what the problem was then, I would come to realize that Danny had borrowed the jewels from the Mob's jeweler with promises to eventually pay for them, but when he couldn't, he would have copies made to appease me. This was well before the invention of cubic zirconia, so you can imagine how poor the imitations were. He was giving me glass.

It wasn't long before I was subpoenaed to appear before a grand jury. I was asked a bunch of rapid-fire questions about Danny Sims, and those questions had my heart pounding. To my surprise, though, none of the questions was related to the Mob. Instead, they all revolved around a guy called Lionel, who was one of Danny's closest friends, and his involvement in the murder of a high-powered Washington official. I knew this particular friend of Danny's very well—we would often travel to DC to parties at the ultra-swank nightclub Lionel owned. Danny would always leave the club with a paper bag full of money, money I never quizzed him about. Whatever he and Lionel were involved in was not my business, and I wanted it to stay that way.

Still, it wasn't the questions about his friend Lionel that put the fear of God in me. Rather, it was the picture the FBI showed me of the gun that had been used in the murder. It looked eerily similar to the gun Danny had been haphazardly loading that day he attacked me in our apartment. That was the first time I had ever seen Danny with a gun, so that image was seared into my brain. So this was why Danny was so afraid—the Mob and Lionel thought that Danny had snitched on them, so they had put a hit on him. Danny needed to put the blame elsewhere, so that's where I came in. He accused me of being the snitch—me, the mother of his child. What a gem of a guy! He didn't need to kill me; he'd have the Mob do it for him.

As I looked at the picture of that gun, I could feel my head begin to throb and my stomach became weak. As soon as I got out of the hot seat, I excused myself. Outside in the hall, I had a long discussion with my lawyer about our next move. Thankfully, my lawyers were already three steps ahead of me and ready to play the wife card. Though Danny and I were in the midst of a divorce, I was still technically his wife and legally not obligated to testify against him about anything. In the end, Danny wouldn't be indicted by the grand jury for co-conspiracy for murder, and no formal charges were filed against him in court.

But that didn't end all of my problems, nor did it change Danny's status with the Mob. He had to stay on the run for the rest of his life, and I was still scared for my life and the lives of my family and friends. The Mob and Lionel would have no way of knowing that I hadn't spoken to the FBI, and they surely still believed Danny's lies about my being the real villain, when in fact it was Danny speaking regularly with the FBI. What could I do now to escape the new kind of hell I was living in? I couldn't go to the police because then I would be dead.

Also, my money was gone, so I couldn't run far even if I wanted to. Danny was well aware of this since he was the one who had spent the cash. And staying with my sister and her family was no longer an option since it put them in jeopardy.

I wouldn't be able to live with myself if anything happened to anyone in my family because I had married a madman, so I ended up taking a room at a seedy hotel in the city (Anansa stayed with Sheilah). Every night I fell on my knees crying and praying to God for strength to make it through the coming weeks and months. I had hit rock bottom.

At the hotel I had plenty of time to think, and after a few days the name Johnny Baylor came to my mind. Johnny, a former special ops ranger, had come to our apartment several times to visit with Danny and to discuss music deals.

Army Rangers are highly trained in general combat and small-unit tactics, as well as unconventional warfare, special reconnaissance, direct action, and counterterrorism. They are the kind of guys who conduct military and paramilitary actions behind enemy lines. In short, Johnny was just the man I needed in my life at that moment.

Johnny used his talents for years with Stax Records, a Tennessee-based label for southern and Memphis soul, and he held several positions on their security team, keeping all the artists, writers, and producers in check. He made sure all disagreements and arguments at the record company were kept to a minimum. I remember Johnny cutting quite the striking figure in our living room, and I was also struck by the complete deference Danny showed him. Danny was seldom in awe of anyone, and I'd never seen him be afraid of any man, but he appeared a bit fearful of Johnny.

Out of the blue one day before Danny and I had split, Johnny called me, offered his number, and suggested I call him if I ever needed his help. I was confused since I was still married and Johnny was involved already with an attractive woman who had accompanied him to the apartment a few times. Apparently, and without my knowledge, news of my ill-fated union was getting around. Johnny was just ahead of the game. Thank goodness he was.

Now I made the call for help, and Johnny and I had dinner to discuss my dire circumstances. We talked about the divorce, the FBI, the Mob, Lionel, and the fears I now had for me and my family. Johnny seemed all too familiar with many of my issues with Danny and willing to help me.

Johnny's first bold move was to call Danny and ask for a meeting. The two met the next day for several hours, and although Johnny never divulged what they talked about, I could only assume that he made it clear to Danny that I hadn't given the FBI any information of any kind involving him or Lionel, and that Danny needed to pass that fact around. Johnny probably also added that he and I were now together, and that if anything should befall me, be it a car accident, robbery, broken leg, or broken nail, Danny would be held directly responsible.

Regardless of whatever Johnny said, I remained concerned for my well-being. Danny was a real fool, so I never knew what to expect from him, but I did feel a certain comfort in Johnny's arrival in my life.

Johnny's second suggestion was a huge one for my sense of security. He invited Anansa and me to move into his fabulous three-bedroom apartment on East Eighty-Ninth Street. I was blown away by his kindness—I had desperately wanted to move Anansa out of my sister's home and bring her to live with me. And I didn't want to stay in that seedy hotel any longer.

As Anansa and I made the move to Johnny's lovely home, divorce proceedings with Danny continued, and the surprises of what really had been going on during my marriage just kept coming. Along with being virtually broke, I also learned that Danny, and only Danny, was earning a large percentage from Elite Model Management and Johnny Casablancas. That bombshell revelation meant Danny had been earning money from each of my modeling assignments while also chipping away at the money I had already made before we met. Johnny Baylor recommended I sue Elite, Danny, Johnny Casablancas, and several advertising companies for conflict of interest and a host of other things done to me and my career over the period of time I was signed with them. I had lost months of work due to the damage done to my reputation as a result of Danny and Johnny Casablancas's sordid and tangled involvement in my career, too.

Johnny Baylor's suggestion of a lawsuit didn't surprise me. He knew a lot about lawsuits, as he had been involved in one with the IRS for over a decade. Johnny made millions over the years at Stax Records from publishing deals, but the IRS wasn't convinced by this explanation of his fortune, hence the lawsuit.

It was clear that with no work coming in I was totally dependent on Johnny. No modeling agency would take me on while I was embroiled in a lawsuit against another one, and going to court would also make my financial situation even bleaker for months to come. But I had to right this incredible wrong done to me. I couldn't just roll over and let people like my former husband and Johnny Casablancas come in and take away everything I had worked for. But there is always a hefty price for fighting back.

Johnny Baylor was the polar opposite of Danny in ways too many to count. He took great pride in his southern background and was good friends with men like Calvin O. Butts, pastor of the Abyssinian Baptist Church in New York City. He loved studying the works of Dr. Martin Luther King Jr., supported the efforts of several black civil rights projects, and was active in a number of other social issues involving race and politics. I learned so much from just being around him.

But though he had volunteered to rescue me from my hell, Johnny was by no means an uncomplicated Prince Charming.

Johnny was a conundrum. A southern gentleman in the most traditional ways, he had been raised to believe that a man never took anything from a woman, and certainly not in the way Danny had stolen from me. Johnny admired how much I had achieved in my work, and abhorred anyone who tried to ruin me along the way. On the other hand, this was the man Danny was afraid of. If I had had the luxury of the time to think more clearly, I might have realized that one day I could end up afraid of him too.

I was getting more and more overwhelmed by all the issues facing me. I hadn't fully recovered from my postpartum depression, either, so the wave of sadness I already felt had now taken an even-tighter grip of me in the midst of my divorce proceedings. Throughout my career, cocaine had been my solace, and as the bottom continued to fall, I welcomed my old friend back with open arms.

Johnny's ultra-chic apartment was so breathtaking—featuring, as it did, sleek chrome fixtures, gorgeous furnishings, and a perfect mix of exotic African art—that it belonged between the covers of some glossy home magazine. Aesthetics aside, it soon became apparent that though the apartment was beautiful, it wasn't exactly child-friendly with its many expensive odds and ends. After about a month of staying with Johnny, he suggested I move in permanently, since he and his girlfriend had pretty much split. I jumped at that idea, but then he also suggested I take Anansa home to my parents' house in Buffalo until I could get my bearings. Johnny felt I needed a clearer picture of what I would be facing as the divorce proceedings continued. I reluctantly agreed and took my baby to my parents for what I thought would be only a limited time.

I had no way of knowing that day, as I left Anansa at my parents, that I'd just made a decision that would haunt and torture me for years to come.

Danny didn't dare touch a hair on my head with Johnny in my life, but Johnny also began playing games of his own, especially regarding Anansa. He kept telling me that my daughter was in the best place with my parents, and that I didn't need to keep calling them every day to check in on her. What I didn't realize was that Johnny was slyly pulling me away from my daughter in hopes of gaining complete control over me. I was living in his house, and was quickly becoming entangled in another man's world and manipulations. This wasn't about my money. Instead, because he was now single and had been helping with my many problems, he felt he deserved my full, undivided attention, and my being a mother to Anansa wouldn't allow that. I was the new woman in his life, and he wanted all of me.

I was too broken to fight Danny in court and Johnny at home. Also, in my heart of hearts, I knew that for the moment at least my baby girl was in the best place with my parents. I was juggling court dates and lawsuits, with no way to even afford my own apartment. As long as Anansa was with my parents, she was in a real home and far from the concrete jungle of New York City. And we would be together again soon.

But if I thought that endlessly navigating the maze that was my life was going to get easier sooner rather than later, I was very mistaken.

Though Johnny never joined me in my bad habits of drugs and drinking, he did smoke about a pack or two of unfiltered Newports a day. Not long after I moved in, he began to notice blood in the sink after brushing his teeth. The news from the doctors was as bad as can be: lung cancer. He had less than six months to live. Johnny took the news like the strong man he was, but I didn't know how much more bad news I could handle in my life. I was in a daze. With everything I was already facing in my own life, I had no idea if I could be strong enough to become the full-time caregiver of someone who was terminally ill. Strangely, you couldn't tell Johnny was sick by looking at him. To his friends and those who didn't know him well, he looked just fine. But at home, he was extremely weak and continued to throw up blood.

Johnny's last girlfriend accompanied him on one doctor's visit at the beginning of his ordeal, but from then on it was just the two of us. Johnny continued to advise me on my legal matters, my divorce, and my lawsuits, and though it may sound strange, it occurred to me that in some ways Johnny believed that by helping me he was also paying penance for some of the questionable things he'd done in the past. He didn't tell me what any of those things were, but it felt to me that freeing me from my hell with Danny was one of his ways of making things right with his maker.

I regularly found myself reading from the Bible during Johnny's illness. My mother had taken us to church every Sunday rain or shine when I was growing up, and during the week we would read various passages from the Bible before heading to bed. Now, for the first time in a long while, God's word became my best friend again, my guiding force. I read the Bible from Genesis to Revelation, from beginning to end, and was amazed by the peace it brought me. I would read the Scriptures aloud to Johnny, too, which I know gave him comfort as he neared his final days. Pastor Butts came over several times a week to pray with us, too.

My need for God didn't circumvent my need to self-medicate, however. I was drinking and taking drugs just as much, if not more, than usual. Johnny was dying right before my eyes, and I hadn't seen Anansa in months—I just didn't know what to do with myself. Though Johnny was ill, I still felt I couldn't go against his wishes and reach out to my daughter or my family. Johnny needed me by his side at all times.

Making matters worse was that I hadn't worked in months because of the legal issues surrounding the divorce. I saw no end to my suffering, so I needed something, anything, to help me forget all the horrific circumstances going so very wrong in my life. Drugs, drinking, and smoking proved the fastest way of getting that done, sometimes in excess.

So I thank my lucky stars that Johnny was there when I nearly overdosed on cocaine. Feeling numb was the only feeling I wanted, but I had gone too far. There isn't anything more frightening than feeling as though you are about to die from overdosing. Even if you've had days when you wished you were dead, when you begin to overdose, your body shakes violently, you begin to sweat profusely, and your heartbeat races so fast you can hear it beating as though it's outside your body. That's exactly what happened to me the day of my overdose. Fortunately, Johnny made me jump into a cold shower with my clothes on and then drink a carton of cold milk.

I know many would say this isn't the best way to save your life in the midst of a drug overdose, but it did save mine, and, I'm sorry to say, more than once.

~

As if all this wasn't bad enough, Danny then decided to instigate a custody battle for my baby girl. He had never showed much interest in his other two children, but now he wanted to challenge me over our child.

It turned out his reasons were far more complicated than I could have imagined.

When I took my daughter to my parents, I honestly assumed all was well, and if there were any problems they would surely find a way to let me know. But without notifying me, a few months after I'd dropped her off, my mother had taken Anansa to stay with my father's sister, Sadie.

Later, my mother would tell me that her reason for sending Anansa away to live with Sadie was that she had to return to work in the wake of my lost earnings. When I was at the height of my career, I sent home a great deal of money to my parents every month. Now that I wasn't working, the money had stopped, and that had apparently made my parents unhappy. They didn't understand the reasons behind my sudden lack of financial assistance, and they seemed to assume that I had brought Anansa to live with them in an effort to blow off my responsibilities. I admit that I hadn't done a great job in explaining my situation to them, but still—to send my baby to my aunt's to live without letting me know was something I'll never understand.

And Sadie, whom my father couldn't stand (and whom as kids *we* couldn't stand), was a true piece of work. In an instant, Anansa became Sadie's calling card for cash. She reached out to me first for money, and when I didn't have any to give to her, her next move was to go to the Devil himself, Danny. And that was when all hell broke loose.

Danny filed for custody of Anansa immediately, and moved forward with a terrible smear campaign in the courts, one that accused me of horrible and dastardly acts. He told the custody judge that during our marriage I had raped his teenage son, given Anansa sleeping pills, and then locked her in the closet. He also told them that I regularly neglected my daughter by leaving her with other people.

Danny's lies just went on and on, and Sadie backed up my ex-husband word for word. I just couldn't believe that someone from my own family would support my ex-husband's horrible and damaging mistruths. My heart broke all over again.

In 1982, the judge decided that Danny had the more appropriate living quarters for Anansa, at our old apartment on Fifth Avenue. He also ruled that since Danny worked mostly from home, he had more time to spend with our daughter and therefore should retain primary custody of her. I was an internationally famous model who traveled all the time, and that didn't help my case at all. I was devastated.

As I grappled with what losing custody of Anansa really meant, Johnny was slipping away from me, too.

I still remember quite vividly the night Johnny died. I was sitting on the edge of our bed; he was in the bathroom. He was very weak, and his voice kept trailing off to the point where I could barely hear him. But I knew that he was in terrible pain, and as he tried to make it back to the bed, there was one phrase I heard very clearly. He said, "I love you." He had never said those words to me before.

I doubt if Johnny had ever said that to many other people in his life, not even to his son, who was the spitting image of him. This was the same son he was determined not to give a cent of his fortune (a fortune that included a stash of about five hundred thousand dollars in cash that he always kept in a golf bag in the bedroom closet).

As Johnny came back into the bedroom, he was covered in sweat, so I told him to lie down so I could change his pajamas and call an ambulance. The paramedics came within ten minutes, but when I showed them into the bedroom, we could see that he was dead.

I collapsed. There is nothing quite like being there to witness someone you love being put in a body bag.

I got myself together by the time the police arrived, but all they did was inform me that, since my name wasn't on the lease, I would need to leave the apartment. You would think with all the crime in New York City the cops would have something better to do than escort a woman out of an apartment the same night her boyfriend died. Whatever—I wasn't leaving without the five hundred thousand dollars. I didn't want the police to take it into evidence. I would have to be slick, as the police's job was to make sure I didn't remove anything but my clothes, so they were following me room to room, and the money would raise a few eyebrows. So I did what any self-respecting woman during the eighties would do. I went into the bedroom closet and pulled out a douche bag and yelled, "I need some privacy—my partner just died."

Nothing clears two males out of a room like the sight of a douche bag. After the cops exited, I put that money in my luggage and made my way to another apartment Johnny owned across town.

Despite Johnny's wishes, I made sure his only son received the bulk of his estate, including the five hundred thousand dollars. I kept the apartment on Eighty-Ninth Street, but his son also received the money from his publishing deals and other property he owned. I never fully understood the issues Johnny had with his son, but in the end I knew what he owned belonged to his only child.

To lose custody of my child, and then to lose Johnny just a few months later, was unbearable. I was filled with grief. Both Danny and Johnny had taken so much from me, and they continued to rob me. I had turned to Johnny to save my life, but had lost everything that mattered as a result.

I thought about suicide many times in the weeks after I lost custody of Anansa. Then I was also faced with having to bury Johnny. I honestly didn't know what I had to live for anymore.

It was the thought of Anansa that stopped me from killing myself. I needed her to know how hard I had fought for her, and how much I loved her. I didn't want to be selfish. Still, some mornings I would have to fight about what I wanted more—to live for my baby girl's sake, or die to be free from my own agony and pain.

Thankfully, not long after Johnny's death, two wonderful things happened.

First, I won my lawsuit against the modeling agency and advertising companies for lost wages and conflict of interest, and was awarded a large settlement. Then, my brother Darren came to live with me on Eighty-Ninth Street. Darren was the real baby of the Johnson family, the youngest of my two brothers and nearly fifteen years younger than me.

Darren had spent about seven years in colleges, and I do mean seven. Many people have a five-year college plan, but Darren was on a seven-year plan. That put considerable strain on my parents, so they reached out to me for help to pay his tuition. I agreed to help him but wanted some assurances that he would graduate that year. He did so, and afterward he decided to come to New York and move in with his big sister.

Having Darren at the house with me was a big boost to my mood during some of those miserable and dark days. I got to know him as a man and not a baby, which was a great experience for both of us. Darren also helped me realize I wasn't going completely crazy as I continued to feel Johnny's considerable presence in the Eighty-Ninth Street apartment. I know many people feel such a thing after they lose someone. For months after Johnny died, I just couldn't shake the feeling that his spirit was everywhere in that house. I could sometimes smell the smoke from one of his Newports, or would catch a whiff of his favorite cologne lingering in the bedroom. I would also catch myself mirroring his same mannerisms by sitting on the edge of the bed the exact same way he did.

This wasn't just wishful thinking, either. Though Darren didn't know Johnny, he also felt the presence of someone else in the apartment. The lights would flicker on and off for no apparent reason, and things would disappear and reappear within days. It was completely strange, but it didn't scare me.

Even with Darren around to brighten my days, I was still hurting badly. I needed the crutches of illegal substances to get me through most days. But I couldn't give in. I soldiered on, and put on my happy face for my daughter when I was able to see her. Then I would go and sink right back into that dark place as soon as I had to take her back to her father's home.

Instead of selling the apartment on Fifth Avenue, as Danny and I were both ordered to do in the divorce proceedings, I agreed to let Danny live there with Anansa so I could walk from Johnny's place, which was just ten blocks away.

Though I had been given court-appointed days to visit with Anansa, Danny agreed to let me see her whenever I wanted. This wasn't out of the kindness of his heart—it was merely so he could flaunt his new lifestyle. He had several girlfriends, whom he would proudly introduce to me whenever I came over. Some were aspiring models, and Danny would ask me to give them advice on their fledgling careers.

But there was worse going on than Danny having girlfriends. One day I walked in and found pornographic flicks playing right in front of Anansa. Other times, I found a bunch of people I didn't know just roaming around. Random men and women in the home couldn't be safe for Anansa at all. On the back of all this, I re-filed for custody but lost again.

I didn't have any proof, and I still don't, but I will always believe Danny paid off a few of those family court judges.

Every time I lost another round of custody hearings, I would go right back into that hole where I drank, smoked, and used cocaine. Also, I wouldn't eat, because I was never hungry, and I ended up weighing ninety-nine pounds. This would have been perfect if I'd been modeling, but I wasn't. For six months I didn't know whether I was going up or coming down; six months where I only left the apartment to see Anansa. I had simply ceased to exist.

Those six months extended to three years and more. I was forever going back and forth to custody court. I was in agony watching Anansa grow up with a father who, though I didn't doubt loved her, was also using her to get back at me.

Still, bit by bit, I could feel my power slowly returning to my spirit and soul. To notify Danny the old me was finally on the way back, I decided that now was the time for us to put the infamous 1215 Fifth Avenue apartment on the market as the divorce court had ordered. That place held so many ugly and painful memories for me that I was sure selling it would be profoundly cathartic.

Never one to allow me to get one up on him, Danny packed up and moved to New Jersey with Anansa after the apartment sold. So I purchased a champagne-colored Mercedes-Benz for the drive. I might as well look stunning during my hour-and-a-half commute to New Jersey.

Though my power was returning in drips, Danny still knew how to push my buttons. Once, while in the New Jersey apartment with Anansa, I recognized a painting given to me by my artist friend Keith Haring. Haring had signed it, "To Beverly, Happy Birthday." I took it home; it was mine, so why not? Danny had been out of town during my visit, and I thought nothing of it. A few days later—I remember it well; I was wearing a wonderful waist-length fur jacket that day—I went back to New Jersey to see my daughter, but when I called up to the apartment from the front desk, Anansa said, "Mommy, don't come up here. I will come down to you."

Several minutes later, the elevator doors opened and two police officers came out. They asked me if I was Beverly Johnson, and when I said yes, they arrested me for theft. It seems that Danny had reported me to the police for taking the Keith Haring picture. He had also worked it out so that the police would be handcuffing me in front of our daughter, but he hadn't counted on our daughter's keen mind. Understanding the game her father was playing, she had kept me from going upstairs to protect me. That was my sweet baby girl.

My arrest was on a Friday, which meant I was looking at a weekend stay in jail if a judge didn't grant me bail. The police finally found a judge in some part of New Jersey who would listen to my story, and once again I found myself explaining the damn fool I'd been married to. Clearly the judge was familiar with this type of story, and he granted me one hundred thousand dollars' bail. Thank goodness Johnny taught me to always keep cash in the house in case of emergencies. I called my assistant Gwen Quinn and told her where the cash was—I always kept a bunch of cash under my bed—and she dutifully rescued me from prison.

Weeks later, the charges were dropped, and the case was thrown out.

But still the madness continued. One day, when Anansa was in the fourth grade, Danny shaved off all her hair. My daughter had had a beautiful head of thick sandy-red, shoulder-length tresses, but he had someone whack it all off. Anansa even ran around for weeks afterward saying, "Look at me, Mommy, I'm a boy."

I took him to court for that, too, because I considered that child abuse. The white judge in the case didn't agree, but anyone with a little black girl would have understood the importance of hair in the African-American community and how it affected a young girl's self-esteem.

My last date with the custody court was something straight out of an episode of *Perry Mason*. That date brought out good ol' Sadie again, and she brought along her fourth or fifth husband, Smitty. All of Sadie's husbands seemed to die early for some reason, and poor, simple Smitty was her latest catch. On a whim, I asked my lawyer to put Smitty on the stand just for the hell of it. Something told me that Smitty would break under pressure, and he would give the court a more honest view of what was really behind Sadie's unwavering dedication to Danny.

I was right. On the stand, Smitty, in tears, told my lawyers that Danny sent them money, bought them a car, and paid for vacations to exotic places, all so that they would paint a less-than-positive portrait of me as a mother. Smitty was sobbing like a baby when he stepped away from the stand. The poor man had a conscience at least, which is more than I could say about my devil aunt. I could feel Sadie huffing, puffing, and spitting pure fire from the back of the courtroom. But the jig was finally up, and the truth was out by the winter of 1987. I felt more than vindicated after years of feeling like the bad guy in a really bad soap opera. The judge didn't change his ruling on the custody issue, but everyone now knew Danny had been lying the entire time.

What I was most in need of back then, though, apart from the truth, was to clean up my act. I had a problem with drinking, smoking, and drugs, but someone needed to shake the hell out of me for me to see how bad off I really was.

The custody battle was over; my daughter was getting older and would be able to make her own decisions about where she wanted to live soon enough. In addition, offers were coming in from the modeling world! It was time to get myself back on track; failure was no longer an option.

CHAPTER 16

Mr. Cosby

I've had my share of close calls with Hollywood directors who've asked me to come in for auditions but wanted much more. The casting couch does, indeed, exist, where these well-known men suggest, ever so politely, that a woman provide personal favors in exchange for landing a role in a film. But usually they allow the woman the freedom to decline.

In 1986, I had a different kind of casting-couch experience.

In the midst of my ongoing custody battle, I was also trying to develop my acting career. The problem was that, as a black actress, I had pretty limited options. Only a few "black movies" were filmed each year, and even fewer television shows featured black characters.

Thankfully there was one huge bright spot for actors of color looking for work. In the world of television, longtime comic Bill Cosby reigned supreme. While growing up in Buffalo in the sixties, I would watch Cosby on *I Spy*, as well as his short-lived TV sitcom *The Bill Cosby Show*. Years later, in September 1984, *The Cosby Show* debuted on NBC and changed television. Cosby played

Cliff Huxtable, a doctor who lives in Brooklyn with his wife, Clair (played by Phylicia Rashad), and five children.

The show's overwhelming popularity and huge ratings put the NBC network back into the television game after years of ranking behind the two other major networks, CBS and ABC. *The Cosby Show* also opened doors for other networks to cast shows with predominantly African-American actors, but still, any black performer worth his salt wanted a guest spot on the show.

That long list included me, so you can imagine my surprise and joy when handlers from the show called to say that Mr. Cosby wanted me to come into the New York studio where the show was filmed to audition for a recurring part as the younger sister of Clair Huxtable. How's that for a lucky break? Although I was beyond thrilled, I was also nervous about revealing my limited comedy skills to the hilarious Mr. Cosby. But I knew I couldn't pass up this golden opportunity to finally get Hollywood's attention.

On my first visit to the set, Mr. Cosby was warm and welcoming. He made sure I met everyone in the cast and crew—I even interrupted Phylicia as she meditated in her dressing room. After the show wrapped up taping, I met Cosby in his office to talk about the role. He asked about my current situation, my divorce, and my custody battle, and also peppered me with questions about my plans for the future and what I hoped to accomplish in a television or film career. I can't describe how it felt to have such a powerful and influential man interested in my life. My luck was finally changing. Mr. Cosby invited me to another taping and suggested I bring my daughter along. I didn't hesitate, because Anansa loved *The Cosby Show*, especially the character Theo, played by Malcolm-Jamal Warner. She thought he was adorable.

After the second taping, Cosby surprised me by inviting me to his home to read for the part. It was a weekend, and I was supposed to spend it with Anansa, per my custody agreement with Danny, but once I told Mr. Cosby that I would have Anansa with me, he quickly said I should bring her along. I'd always heard that Cosby's brownstone was a sight to behold, with its spacious floor plan and a remarkable collection of African-American art, so I was excited to go.

When we arrived at Cosby's Lenox Hill home that Saturday afternoon, his staff served us a lovely brunch. Anansa spilled her glass of orange juice all over the floor, and Mr. Cosby seemed a tad miffed about that, but thankfully the staff swiftly moved in to clean it up.

A tour of the gorgeous home followed, and we had the chance to meet Ennis, Mr. Cosby's only son (Ennis was tragically murdered in Los Angeles just a few years later). While I had a lovely visit, there was no opportunity that day to practice scenes for the show, so when Mr. Cosby invited me to visit a few days later to run a few lines, I agreed.

On that next visit, we started by sharing a meal, and then set off to practice our lines in the second floor's bar area. The first thing to catch my eye was an enormous espresso machine sitting on the bar's counter. Espresso machines weren't common in homes in the mid-eighties.

As we settled in to rehearse, Mr. Cosby asked if I wouldn't mind acting out the part of a drunken woman for the scene we were about to practice. As I concentrated on portraying the best drunk I could, Mr. Cosby made a cappuccino and offered it to me. I declined—it was late afternoon, and coffee of any kind would keep me from sleeping that night. Between the custody court battles and a host of other issues in my life, I really needed every possible minute of sleep and it often took me hours to drift off.

But Mr. Cosby wasn't interested in my insomnia. He kept insisting that I'd never had a cappuccino like this one, and I'd be missing out on something really spectacular. I didn't want to argue with him after he'd been so gracious, so against my better judgment I took a few sips. In an instant, I felt woozy. I certainly had enough experience with mood enhancers to know the way they make you feel, and the room had begun spinning around me. Mr. Cosby motioned for me to come over to him, and somehow I steadied myself enough to make my way across the room to where he was standing. As we met in the center of the room, he put his hands around my waist, and I put my hand on his shoulder to ensure I wouldn't fall down.

All of a sudden, the impact of what was happening to me really set in and I became enraged. I believed that Mr. Cosby had drugged me. Before I knew it, a profanity-laced tirade came out of my mouth. I called him "motherfucker" so many times he stepped back and glared at me as if I were losing my mind.

As I began to wobble even more, Mr. Cosby grabbed my arm and dragged me roughly down the stairs. Before I could say anything, he had thrown me into a cab and slammed the door behind me. Somehow, I found the lucidity to tell the cabdriver where I lived before I completely passed out. I can only assume my lovely doorman made sure I reached my apartment safely, since he'd helped me out a few times before. I woke up late the next day still woozy and confused about what had happened. What had Bill Cosby tried to do to me and why?

Later, I decided to call Mr. Cosby and ask him what had happened. I used the number he had given me, and his wife, Camille, answered. She told me that she and Bill were both in bed, and that was that. I never called him again. I had too much to lose to pursue it. I would have to make my own peace with it somehow.

I've seen Mr. Cosby once or twice since that day, although he did not speak to me on either occasion.

Fast-forward to December 2014. A comic doing his stand-up routine accused Cosby of rape, and a recording of that performance went viral. As odd as it may seem, that comedy routine inspired more than twenty women to come forward to say they had been drugged and/or raped by Bill Cosby. In the end it took nearly thirty some years before I felt strong enough to share my story with the public, a decision largely influenced by the bravery of those women telling their truth. I felt a tremendous weight lifted from my entire being. I never knew that I was carrying so much pain from that one day thirty years ago. I can honestly say that speaking out was one of the best decisions I've ever made in my life and the best thing I could ever have done for myself and other women who have faced similar circumstances. I was so afraid of talking about what had happened to me for so long that I was truly shocked by the amazing response I received. I can only hope that telling my story gives courage to other women to speak out about the trauma that they have faced.

CHAPTER 17

Iron Mike and the Real Fresh Prince of Bel-Air

One day, in November 1986, someone rang my doorbell at my Eighty-Ninth Street apartment. It was a tranquil Sunday afternoon, and as I wasn't expecting anyone, I didn't exactly rush to answer it. When I finally made it to the door, I asked who was there, and a slightly high-pitched voice on the other side answered.

"It's Mike Tyson," said the voice.

About a week earlier, right before Mike was set to fight for the first time for the heavyweight championship title in Las Vegas, my dear friends Paul Herman and Nikki Haskell had introduced Mike and me at an uptown eatery in New York City. Paul had said that I was in the presence of the next heavyweight champion of the world, even if he did look like one big kid.

As soon as we met, Mike gushed about what a big a fan he had always been of me and my career. He wouldn't stop telling me how beautiful I was, and I admit that I basked in the sincerity of his compliments. As we got ready to leave, Mike asked if it would be OK if he bothered Paul for my number; he wanted us to go out on a date sometime soon if possible. I hadn't been dating much over the last few years, but there was no reason I couldn't begin again, and there was no time like the present. I'd been celibate for a while, too, so I was more than ready for that to come to an end.

Mike was almost fifteen years my junior, but I was in need of a good time for a change, and I could tell Mike was surely capable of giving me that. I had only had one short encounter around that time—it wasn't a relationship—with comedian Eddie Murphy, and that hadn't gone well. It was early in Eddie's success, and man, was he full of himself! I had thrown a party at Mr. Chow, the swank eatery on the Upper East Side, and Eddie had brought his bodyguards with him, which was bad enough—what was worse was that he invited them to sit down and eat, too. You don't have your bodyguards sit down and eat at Mr. Chow alongside Mick Jagger and other celebrities. Even worse, those same bodyguards also went into the bathroom and told Mick Jagger to leave so Eddie could use the bathroom by himself. Can you believe that? Needless to say, that romantic connection ended very quickly.

Mike Tyson was an entirely different case. He began calling me the very day we met. I enjoyed our talks; they made me feel young and vibrant again after four years of going to hell and back. Mike was a pure blast—I just loved being around his energy. He was always so charged up and ready to go.

Along with discussions about life, we also talked about his upcoming fight in Las Vegas, and whether or not he had a solid chance of winning. If he did win, he would become the youngest heavyweight champion in history, which was a very big deal. I assured him he would win, but what did I know really? At one point during one of our long conversations, when the talk veered toward us going out on a date, I said words that even surprised me as they came tumbling out of my mouth.

"If you win," I said, "I'll give you some."

I have no idea what I was thinking when I said such a thing. I couldn't have been thinking straight. Mike was completely silent for a few seconds; I think he was genuinely stunned by what I just offered him.

Then he replied, "OK, deal."

Days later, on November 22, 1986, Mike stepped into the ring with Trevor Berbick at the Las Vegas Hilton for what fight promoters had billed "Judgment Day." Tyson dominated Berbick from the opening bell, and won the title with a second-round knockout.

At just twenty years and four months old, Mike Tyson was the world's youngest heavyweight champion.

I was so elated for Mike. He had endured so much pain and trauma as a kid that to see him win on such a huge stage was wonderful to behold.

Nineteen hours later, Mike Tyson was standing at my front door on Eighty-Ninth Street. I'm not sure if he had taken the red-eye on Delta, chartered a private plane, or borrowed Dorothy's ruby slippers and clicked them to make a wish, but whatever he did had gotten him to my apartment within hours of winning the biggest fight of his young life.

I had made him a promise, and he obviously wanted to make sure I fulfilled it. Our first time together was nice, if not the most passionate of nights I'd experienced with a man. Mike was young and still learning how to please a woman, but I very much enjoyed it anyway. Mike was so full of excitement and vigor that it was actually contagious.

For many weeks and months to come, we had a lot of fun. Mike was the toast of the town with his new heavyweight champ title, and I began to introduce him to many in the high society of New York. He loved every minute of it. This was not a world he had ever imagined becoming a part of given his background as a child. (By the time he was thirteen years old, Mike had been arrested thirty-eight times for a series of petty crimes.)

One night, he fingered a diamond necklace I was wearing, looked me straight in the eye, and said, "This is pretty. There was a time when I would have snatched it off your neck. But I don't think that way anymore."

Mike grew up poor, and wasn't sure who his real father was, and kids in school had made fun of his high-pitched voice and lisp. His mother had died when he was sixteen years old, and that was when boxing trainer Cus D'Amato and his wife became his legal guardians.

Mike told me an amazing story about the time Muhammad Ali came to speak at D'Amato's gym one year. Mike was still a young boy, and Ali had patted him on the head as he passed him by. Mike had never considered taking up boxing before that day, but just one touch by the greatest boxer that ever lived set him on his own history-making path.

But despite our connection, I wasn't exactly broadcasting our romantic involvement. This was nearly thirty years ago, years before Ashton and Demi and the whole cougar trend. There was nothing cute, sexy, or attractive about being a cougar in 1986, and I knew that all too well. In truth, I'm not certain there's anything cute about it today, given the end result of many of those younger male/older female affairs.

But for the moment, I was having fun. I was enjoying the thrill of watching Mike walk right into all that fame and fortune the way he did, like a little kid having the time of his life.

Anansa, too, just loved Mike to pieces, and he adored her right back. I'll never forget the weekend he flew both of us to Buffalo because he wanted to meet my family. That was the kind of guy Mike was. He was always so fascinated by the people in his life, and he always wanted to know more about them and where they came from. He wanted to meet my parents and my siblings to find out more about what made me tick. I took him to meet my best friend, Dada, and every time we left the house they damn near threw him a ticker-tape parade.

～

Mike was a true hero to the average guy who had been knocked down time and time again by life. With his heavyweight win in Vegas, he had been able to prove that he could get up and succeed. But it was not without its problems. When I took Mike by the local barbershop in Buffalo, some idiot decided he wanted to pick a fight with Mike for no good reason. I loved how Mike was able to just walk away from that fool without engaging him at all. Mike knew how far he had come and how much he had to lose.

After a few weeks, Mike took me to the Catskills to meet Cus's wife. Cus was dead by this time, but it was fabulous to meet the woman who had taken on the role of surrogate mother in Mike's life. I could tell she approved of our friendship because I think she could tell I wasn't out to take advantage of Mike. I learned a lot about Mike by visiting the home where he'd spent much of his late teens. In his room, there were still tapes of fights by legends like Jack Johnson, Muhammad Ali, Larry Holmes, George Foreman, Leon Spinks, and many others. He had studied them constantly, and had learned every boxing move. He took his craft seriously. Mike was much smarter than most people ever gave him credit for, and over the years that served him well.

I'm sure our families knew we were dating, but no one really said anything, so our love life was still pretty low-key. I didn't need ridicule or judgment about any of my decisions at this point in my life. I just wanted to have a good time with a man who seemed to enjoy being with me. Mike didn't have an agenda, either, from what I could tell, and that alone endeared him to me very much.

That said, there were moments when I felt more like his mother, and goodness how I hated those feelings! One evening, over dinner at Mr. Chow in New York, he was drinking so much champagne that I couldn't stop myself from asking him to slow down. He responded by opening his mouth wide to reveal that it was filled with food, just like a kid would do. I couldn't do anything but laugh. When I felt uneasy about that part of our relationship, Mike would sense it and calm me down by singing me the Ready for the World song "Love You Down."

> *It never really mattered too much to me*
> *That you were just too darned old for me.*
> *All that really mattered was you were my girlfriend.*

Mike couldn't sing worth a damn, but he made his point and I loved it.

Eventually, reality set in, and Mike's fame began to open doors for him to meet other women. We continued to see each other here and there and enjoy evenings together, but I could tell the initial thrill was gone.

At one point, Mike began dating Naomi Campbell, which didn't bother me because I knew how that was going to turn out. I'd been around Naomi enough to know her taste in men, and Mike didn't exactly fit, no matter his fame or fortune.

For example, at one event I had overheard Naomi in a heated exchange with Robert De Niro (her beau at the time) during which she demanded he buy her a building. A building—I love Naomi! That girl knows how to ask for what she wants, and I'm sure she gets it most of the time. But Mike wasn't that guy, and more than likely he was never going to become that guy. Theirs was a short-lived affair; Mike even called me a few times to discuss it, and I just listened as a friend would do.

But my heart would break the next time he wanted to talk about a lady friend. Mike called me up to tell me that he was madly in love, was ready to get married, and wanted my approval.

The woman's name was Robin Givens, and he wanted me to say it was OK.

It wasn't OK, not just because I had feelings for him—I did— but because I also knew Robin. I won't disparage her here; I don't have to, since it's well documented how that particular love match between Mike and Robin turned out. Suffice to say it was a horrible nightmare for Mike in every way possible.

But Mike didn't want to hear the cold, hard truth about the woman he wanted to marry, so I didn't give it to him. Instead, I told him that if he was in love, he should follow those feelings wherever they led him. Mike had other friends who did try to tell him to run the other way from Robin, but he didn't heed their advice.

My mother told me much later on in my life that she knew both Billy and Danny were wrong for me, but she also knew I was in love with them and that meant I was going to marry those men no matter what anyone said to me. I would just have to learn for myself. It was the same with Mike Tyson.

I didn't hear from Mike for a long while after his marriage to Robin ended. I assumed he was too embarrassed to even discuss it, particularly that infamous Barbara Walters interview where he seemed comatose and heavily medicated. I never believed he was bipolar, for the record. Maybe Mike was depressed, but who the hell isn't depressed from time to time in this life?

It didn't take Mike long to break my heart yet again after his divorce from Robin. This time it was over the 1991 rape allegations. That rape case divided the black community and captured national headlines. Many in the black community sided with Mike, choosing to place the blame on the eighteen-year-old-girl. But even though I loved Mike to pieces, I wasn't in the room that night with the two of them and have no clue what actually happened. The hospital reports said the girl's physical condition was consistent with that of someone who had been raped, and as a woman, I had to accept and respect that finding for what it was, the very same way I would want it accepted and respected for me, or my daughter, or my granddaughter.

I hated to see Mike go to jail and lose years of his life behind bars, but like it or not, very bad decisions had been made. What I really regretted was that there hadn't been anyone around him to guide him away from danger. Mike needed people around him who would prevent him from getting caught in the wrong places with the wrong people at the wrong time. When you're at his level of stardom, there are so many people wanting things from you that it's important to have someone watching your back. It's so easy to make a misstep and screw up your entire life. And Mike Tyson never had that someone.

I didn't speak to Mike during the years he was in prison, or for years after he was released—our paths simply didn't cross. I winced at the news of his biting Holyfield's ear, and at the numerous bankruptcies. The large tattoo on his face confused and saddened me, too, as did the death of his four-year-old daughter.

Yet Mike continues to thrive, with Broadway plays, HBO specials, and bestselling books. I glory in that. When he was sentenced to jail more than twenty years ago, I wasn't sure where Mike would end up. I worried how he would fare under such trying circumstances after the troubled childhood he'd had. To see that he has emerged even stronger after so many battles has cheered my heart. He was a fearless kid, a brave young fighter, and an even stronger man. I'm more proud of him than ever.

The next man in my life would prove to be much more of a conundrum than Mike. His name was Benny, and the story of his teen years were used as the basis of the popular nineties show starring Will Smith, *The Fresh Prince of Bel-Air*.

Benny was the son of a well-known jazz drummer, Ahmad Medina, and he grew up in the ritzy 90210 zip code, where he attended Beverly Hills High School. There, he met Kerry Gordy, son of famous Motown founder Berry Gordy, and they became fast friends. Benny would often spend nights at the Gordy home, and those years of hanging out with one of the richest African-American families in Beverly Hills seemed perfect for prime-time television. The show began filming while Benny and I were dating, and I watched in awe as it became a bona fide hit.

Jane Fonda's current boyfriend, Richard Perry, introduced me to Benny in 1988. At the time I was traveling back and forth from New York to Los Angeles and considering a full-time move to the West Coast (the sunshine and palm trees were calling my name). Richard and I had been hanging out together for weeks, and when he left town for a while, he often asked Benny to keep me company. Before I knew it, Benny and I really began to connect, though Richard was none too pleased about it when he returned.

Benny and I quickly became an item for a number of reasons, but one of the major ones was the way his creative mind worked. I loved to watch him do his thing in the studio, particularly since he'd learned so much under the watchful eye of the master Berry Gordy. Under Gordy, Benny wrote and produced for Motown acts such as Teena Marie, Rick James, Billy Preston, and the Temptations. It couldn't get any better.

Benny's positive energy was so addictive and brought out the best in me. I was still trying to climb my way out of the hole I'd found myself in since my divorce and everything else that had happened. He encouraged me to formulate my own ideas for television. I had an early blueprint for *America's Next Top Model* and shared it with Benny. I even registered the idea with the Writers Guild, but I let it lapse, so I can't blame anyone else but myself for losing it.

(Benny would later manage Tyra Banks, who had a major hit with the idea.)

Benny got me going in other ways as well. Our personal chemistry was off the charts—we couldn't keep our hands off each other in private or public, and he was the best kisser I'd ever known, and that is saying a lot.

At Dan Tana's, our favorite swanky old-school restaurant in Los Angeles, we would just sit in a red booth and kiss while other guests ate dinner. Soon, I was an overnight regular at Benny's gorgeous home, and together we threw the most talked-about parties. Since this was right in the middle of *Fresh Prince* being taped, Anansa would fly out to Los Angeles to watch the tapings with her friends and have a ball playing with all the new electronic gadgets Benny would buy for her. He loved giving me the finest in clothes and jewels from all around the world, too—he was quite the man. It wasn't long before Benny and I were head over heels, spending all our free time with each other, and there was talk of us moving in together and maybe marriage down the line.

One weekend in 1988, I decided to spend a few weeks living with Benny just to get a feel of how it would be. The first night after I moved in, Benny didn't even come home. He'd never done that before in all the nights we'd spent together. I was livid! For some reason, Benny spending all night out opened my eyes to the harsh reality that the two of us just didn't mesh on a basic level.

Soon, there began to be too many other unanswered questions about our relationship, and I was becoming more frustrated by all of it. Unfortunately, I've always been a sucker for a sad face and a good sob story. Benny begged me not to leave or break it off, so we tried again. I guess I didn't want to let go of him either—I wanted a love that was solid and didn't fall apart like too many of my other relationships.

In fact, I wanted a happy ending so much that we traveled as far as the Ritz-Carlton in Dana Point, California, to get married just a few months later. But my good sense kicked in and I backed out the night before because I knew it wouldn't and couldn't last. I already had two marriages that had failed, and I didn't need a third.

In the end, I realized we both loved high drama. That was good for a movie, but not for a marriage. Benny begged me to change my mind again on our ride back to Los Angeles, but I knew I'd had enough heartache over the years to walk away this time before the real pain set in. That said, I needed quite a bit of therapy to aid me in getting over Benny.

I saw Benny again just a few years ago, and he tried to rekindle our romance by using that same charm he'd used the first time we fell in love. He wanted to fly me to a Jennifer Lopez concert in Paris right then and there on his private plane (Benny manages her), and I'll admit I was very tempted to throw caution to the wind and join him. But a voice in my head kept whispering, Be smarter this time and protect your heart. Too much time had gone by to go back down memory lane with Benny. When some doors close, they should remain that way.

CHAPTER 18

Victory Is Mine!

Finally, the custody battle for my daughter, which had nearly taken all of my strength, was over.

The truth coming out in court about all the lies Danny had told didn't overturn the custody ruling, but it did allow Anansa to come to live with me full-time when and if she wanted. I was sure my daughter would want to at some point. My name had been cleared, and Danny's tales about me had been exposed for what they were: hateful lies. It wasn't everything that I wanted, but it was as good as I was going to get for the moment.

Now I had one last major battle to wage, and it was the epic battle of battles because it was the battle with myself. After years of self-loathing and self-destruction, I needed to get better physically so that I could truly enjoy my life, but to do that I needed to confront and accept that something was wrong inside.

For years, I had been walking around in a semiconscious daze, thinking both my physical and mental health were fine, when in fact they weren't. I could manage sobriety long enough to put on a good front for the days I saw Anansa while she was living with Danny, but now I needed to be completely healthy for the day that Anansa came to live with me.

～

With my beloved James sadly gone from my life, God saw fit to send me another guru in the form of Quintin Yearby. Quintin, the young boyfriend of the designer Fernando Sánchez, made it his personal mission to get me back on the runway and into the modeling game.

The business had done a complete 360 since I had left the building. New people, new places, and an array of new faces had come aboard to claim their spot as new muses of famous designers, and to star in the pages of the glossy fashion magazines.

The reigning face was Iman's, and I was already very familiar with her. In my absence, she had become the proverbial toast of Madison Avenue in both print and runway modeling. Iman had gone through what I heard was a very difficult divorce from Spence Haywood, too, and her marriage had been filled with many of the same things I'd faced with Danny. But she hadn't allowed it to slow her down. Now I was ready to do the same.

I so wanted back into the modeling game. Fashion and modeling had been my only way of life, and my newfound friend Quintin was determined to see me reclaim my rightful place at the top of the modeling world. He called me constantly, asking me to appear as a runway model in a show for his boyfriend Fernando's first couture collection. At first I declined his invitations because I wasn't interested in doing a runway show—it didn't matter who the designer was. I had more than enough money from my settlement to just sit back and ponder long and very hard the when, the where, and the how of the way I wanted to reemerge on the world modeling stage.

But the more I chatted with Quintin (because he wouldn't stop calling), the more I found myself softening my attitude, until gradually it shifted to *when* my return should be, not if. Quintin was now filling the shoes my dear James once wore. There was a time when I thought no one could ever replace my James, but I loved Quintin's spirit and vibe.

Quintin was no carbon copy of James, though. Quintin had much more spice in his personality, whereas my beloved James was more refined, more dignified. There was only one James—he had class and style like I'd never seen before. Forty years on, I can still say I've never met anyone like James Farabee. How I still miss him.

—

Eventually, Quintin convinced me that my career had been on hold long enough and that his darling boyfriend's couture showing was just the right venue to begin my return to the forefront of fashion.

Fernando Sánchez had become a designer with a lot of buzz around town. His designs introduced dressmaking techniques to silky slips and caftans so they could easily transcend their functional limitations. He had trained at the École de la Chambre Syndicale de la Couture in Paris (one of his classmates had been Yves Saint Laurent). Laurent went on to introduce the modern concept of "ready" that revolutionized the way women dressed in their everyday lives. Sánchez caused his own revolution by changing the way women dressed in their sleep. (Saint Laurent would later hire Sánchez to design lingerie for his company.)

With my return to the runway in the works, I tried not to become overly obsessed with my appearance for my first big show since my self-imposed exile. It had been about three or four years since I'd done a runway, and I was sure I looked pretty good—I always looked pretty good—but was I model/runway fabulous? I just didn't know.

One lesson I was forced to learn while living with Johnny was how to become less concerned with my appearance. As a model, you live and die by your own reflection. Our faces and bodies are our bread and butter, so we rarely pass a mirror without pausing to gaze into it. Johnny had once told me that, yes, I was beautiful, and, yes, my beauty had value on Madison Avenue, but in the real world, beauty meant only so much and only lasted so long. He added that men ultimately only wanted one thing from a woman, and in the end would take it from *any* woman, no matter how beautiful.

In essence, Johnny was saying my beauty really wasn't so special after all. According to him, my looks only gave me a slight advantage over women working nine to five. After that, my tendency to look in the mirror every time I could pretty much ended. I found myself focusing on more pressing issues, and I had more than enough of those to keep me busy. It felt so good—no, it felt *great* not to have to be consumed with the superficial 24-7.

Beauty is indeed its own beast, and its own burden, when you have no reprieve from it. But now I had decided to get back into the thick of things, so a few superficial thoughts here and there were to be expected.

~

Fernando Sánchez's show was held in late August, just before the more well-known designers debuted their collections for the seasons. Though Fernando wasn't a top designer, he was definitely one to watch, so all the fashion press flocked to his studio that late summer day to see his first couture collection. My appearance in the show was top secret, which helped my preshow jitters just a bit.

Backstage getting ready, I could feel the steely stares of the other models and hear the whispers, "Where has she been?" No one said anything to me personally, because that would have required too much empathy. That said, one makeup artist did dare to ask how I was holding up as she applied my foundation. I could tell she was really asking about my life generally, and I desperately wanted to answer in the calmest, most straightforward way possible to show everyone how strong I was and would always be. Instead, as I began to speak, tears streamed down my cheeks, and the team of makeup artists immediately had to turn on fans to stop my entire made-up face from sliding off. Needless to say, that was the last makeup artist to ask me a question before a show.

Fernando decided I would open the show in his gorgeous orange, one-shoulder taffeta design. I closed my eyes, said a quick prayer as the curtains parted, and proceeded to walk purposefully down the long catwalk. I could hear a few gasps as I did my strut, which threw me off a bit because I wasn't sure whether they were the audience's reaction to seeing me or the clothes. In any other world, a woman standing five-foot-nine and weighing barely a hundred pounds would produce a reaction of pure shock and horror, but in the world of fashion I was the picture of health and the ideal of beauty.

By the time I reached the end of the stage, I was sure the reaction from the crowd was two thumbs up and a gold star. It was confirmed the next day when the press reviews of the show, the clothes, and of me, all sang our praises to the highest heavens. I was on the top of the fashion world again, and it felt so good! With one short walk down the catwalk in Fernando's show, I had reclaimed my rightful place.

Within days, Calvin, Ralph, and Halston were ringing my phone again like the good old days, personally asking me to be in their fall shows. I could not believe all the love I was receiving after what felt like years of isolation and defeat. It felt damn good to be wanted and needed by all the fashion kings once more, and I said yes to each and every one.

At the Calvin Klein show a few weeks later, the room was all abuzz with talk of which model would close the show. Opening or closing a designer's show was a major honor, and Iman had been Calvin's muse for the last few years. Once upon a time, that had been me, but things change.

That year—1988—at Calvin's request I would be the one closing the show instead of Iman. I was the hot girl once again, so of course Calvin would use me to close the show. It was good for his business, and this was all about business. And I hoped that Iman would understand.

But I thought wrong. The Calvin Klein show that year would mark the first time in years I would be seeing my old friend, and I was so looking forward to saying hello to her and reconnecting after losing touch. This business about closing the show would mean nothing between two black women who walked through the fire a few times over the years. I couldn't imagine Iman would give two damns about who closed or opened Calvin's car door, much less a fashion show, after all we'd been through.

Sadly, when Ms. Iman arrived at the venue that day, she walked off the elevator, looked me dead in the face, and turned away as though she hadn't seen me at all.

I was mortified, but figured that maybe she hadn't seen me. Later, we were all getting dressed and I saw her again, and damn if she didn't do the same exact thing.

"You've got to be kidding!" I said out loud. "Homegirl is tripping."

I was too angry to be hurt, and too angry to think straight. Before she could walk away the second time, though, I grabbed her by the arm and pulled her into a side room.

What happened next I'm not completely proud of, but I did it so I'll own up to it.

"What the fuck is wrong with you?" I said. "How dare you pass me like you don't see me? Don't you understand how crazy that makes us both look? Don't you know people see you doing that to me? I'm not your enemy, and you are not my enemy."

I obviously scared the hell out of Iman that day because she never passed me again without speaking. We even began hanging out again for a while, but that didn't last long. She met David Bowie soon after, and the rest is history.

~

Unfortunately, my once-again booming modeling career couldn't be the primary focus of my life as it had been once upon a time. I was a mother now, and trying to reenter the world of full-time motherhood was an adjustment. Anansa would need some time to wean herself from the wayward life she had been living with her father, and I wanted her to have that time and space. It would be a slow transition, and she needed to have the freedom to come to live with me whenever she wanted, when she was ready.

Though she had been forced to grow up fast, she was still a young child, and I knew she couldn't fully appreciate how much of a pawn she had been in the game her father had been playing with me. This was a man who made deals to have his daughter married off to some African prince when she became a teenager. What father would do that to his only daughter in this modern era?

At one point after the custody case ended, Danny took Anansa on an extended trip to South Africa. Who knew if he would ever bring my child back to the United States and to me? According to the custody ruling, he wasn't even allowed to take her so many miles away from the city of New York, and certainly not out of the country.

It turned out that Danny wanted to move to South Africa to open a massive recording studio and capitalize on the burgeoning music scene there. My guess is he was also running from his issues in the States. As luck would have it, I was invited to South Africa by a number of organizations, particularly the lavish Sun City resort and hotel. The resort paid for me and my new assistant to fly over for a couple of weeks, and the timing couldn't have been more perfect because I wanted my baby girl back home.

I hadn't traveled to South Africa before because of apartheid. I had been asked to appear in a Dial soap ad in the late seventies for a whopping million dollars, but I refused to do anything until Nelson

Mandela was released from prison and apartheid had come to an end. I was also asked to pose for the cover of *Town and Country* magazine in South Africa, but my response was the same.

But now the situation was different for me, too. I had to travel to South Africa and check on my baby girl.

There was racial tension even on the flight to South Africa. The attitude from the crew and other passengers was unbelievable. At one point I was made to use the bathroom at the back of first class when the one in the front was closer. I was one of the few blacks on the flight; even my assistant was white. The stares and glares I received were completely unnerving—I couldn't believe this was really the late eighties and this kind of idiocy still existed.

My time visiting the South had prepared me for this world. My Mother Dear taught me the best lesson on how to defer to white people when I visited my grandparents' land in Florida. I was about nine years old and we were standing in line at the grocery store one day when suddenly a white woman cut in front of us. The up-from-the-north Yankee in me immediately said to the lady, "Excuse me, miss, we were in line first."

My Mother Dear quickly silenced me by saying, "That's OK," to the lady. I didn't understand at first—I was angry, upset, hurt, and embarrassed by what this woman had just done to us.

But what my Mother Dear knew well was that this woman was to be pitied in every way. Anybody who could so easily disrespect the basic rights of another human being had their own demons to face, and confronting her in that moment would do little good.

Stares and shoves and being forced to use a different bathroom were only a preview of the bad behavior I would experience once I landed in South Africa. I was on a black continent, and the disrespect and contempt I encountered was astounding.

At the airport and the hotel, white employees wouldn't even look me in the eye while checking my bags. The valet barely acknowledged me, and it was the same with the front desk at the hotel. It took my praying to God for strength and patience to allow me to see the love in all the people around me.

~

Sun City was a luxury casino and resort situated in the North West Province of South Africa. It was only a two-hour drive from Johannesburg and was considered a key entertainment venue in South Africa at the time, welcoming performers such as Frank Sinatra, Queen, Rod Stewart, and Elton John.

But the resort wasn't without its share of harsh critics. In 1985, activist and producer Steven Van Zandt founded a group to protest apartheid in South Africa. The group produced the song "Sun City," which urged musicians not to perform at the resort, suggesting that to do so would be an acceptance of racism and apartheid.

After arriving in Johannesburg, I headed straight to Danny's home, which was one massive, sprawling mansion. Anansa had already been enrolled in one of the finest schools in the area, and Danny seemed to want to stay there for a while. But I was determined that my daughter wouldn't be joining him permanently. Common sense, however, didn't appeal to Danny, so he didn't budge, and he refused to give me Anansa's passport.

I was done with custody battles, so there was very little I could or would do, and Danny knew it. But fate would intervene before my trip was done. Though I didn't know how I would get my daughter back home, I decided to make the most of the two weeks in South Africa by going on safaris with Anansa and doing as much sightseeing as we could. It felt so natural to be in the motherland and among people with skin that so closely resembled my own. What beautiful land, customs, and people! It was the trip of a lifetime and a great opportunity to teach Anansa about our heritage and culture. The stories were all around us, and I could see and hear them in the faces of the people that passed me by on the street, and in the shapes of the buildings. Anansa and I bonded over hot-air balloon rides over the city, fireworks celebrations, and the best music concerts ever, at Sun City. I loved every minute of my time with Anansa there, but it couldn't last. I needed to get back home and wanted her to come with me. There was no way for me to make frequent trips back and forth to South Africa given the cost. Danny and I would have to find a compromise.

My compromise was simple—Anansa had to come home.

~

One night, I arrived at the hotel frazzled, not to mention very late, to a reception held by a high-ranking woman with close ties to the African National Congress. Arriving late anywhere is incredibly rude, but being late is one of the worst forms of disrespect you can display toward the host of any event in South Africa.

The host wouldn't even speak to me for the first thirty minutes or so, and remained in a back room handling other business. At one point, I was escorted back to see her, and after apologizing profusely for my tardiness, I immediately launched into the story of my daughter and how she'd been taken away from me.

I couldn't tell if my story was registering at all, but after a while her body language shifted slightly and she began to nod as if she understood exactly what I was saying. Other women in the room began nodding their heads, too, and speaking in low voices in a language I didn't understand.

I had no idea how much that night would change my circumstances for the better with my ex-husband.

The next day I went to visit Anansa. When I got there, Danny opened the door and handed her passport to me as soon as I walked in. I didn't ask any questions or say anything—instead, I just took the passport and helped my baby girl pack her things. We were going home! Praise the Lord!

I was told some time later by those in the know that the ANC and the women who worked with it had a lot of power, and were none too pleased to hear of Danny's globe-trotting ways with my daughter. They made their displeasure known to my ex-husband in very clear terms that even he understood, and demanded that he return my daughter instantly.

I took my daughter back to New York a few days later, and Danny dutifully found his way back there over the next few months, too. Anansa continued to move between our two households—she still needed time to decide where she wanted to be, and I was content to wait as long as she needed to make the decision.

Since I was celebrating the return to my career, and the fact that Anansa was beginning to see the truth about her father, I decided to try to see family and old friends again, people I'd shut out of my life at my lowest moments and now needed to see more than anything.

~

One face I really wanted to get up close and personal with again was Grace Jones's. We had only met once at a roller rink, but I knew that if we were to ever spend time together, much fun would be had. We both had children around the same age. Grace had a son named Paulo Goude, and he and Anansa often had a ball playing together in New York. Everything about Grace inspired me to keep moving forward and away from the gloom and doom of the years past. I needed to reinvent myself, and no one could deny that Grace was the master of reinvention, not to mention of self-esteem.

Most women should be lucky to have the type of confidence that Grace displayed. And just having Grace's slightly manic energy around me was a real boost for my morale. Plus, Grace loved nothing more than a good party, and I loved nothing more than giving one!

But that's not all we had in common. Since we both started

out as models, we shared a few very bad habits, too. Sadly, my self-medicating ways hadn't quite gone away. Being sober around Anansa, whom I was spending more and more time with, was no problem, and I was similarly careful when I was working. Only when I was alone in my apartment did I fall victim to those dangerous vices again.

I still didn't believe I had a real problem, but a big hint was on its way.

~

The hint came in the form of my old friend Alicia Melkon, who called me from Paris, where she lived. She was concerned about her daughter, Gigi, who she was certain had joined some type of crazy cult. She had gotten this idea because Gigi had begun to recite a number of strict rules by which to live.

Gigi lived in Los Angeles, but regularly traveled to New York for work, so Alicia asked if I would have a heart-to-heart with her to find out more about what was going on in her life.

When Gigi came to New York, I threw a party at my swank high-rise and filled it with libations and many other substances. I had much more than my share of good times that night, and the next morning, as I tried to deal with my daily hangover, which included a splitting headache among other things, Gigi asked me, "Have you ever thought of getting sober?"

What in the world was this girl talking about?

Then Gigi opened up about her troubles with addiction and how she had sought help through various AA programs (the "cult" her mother was worried about). Gigi's brutal honesty with me that morning hit me hard. But I still wasn't ready. I needed something more to push me to get real help.

~

My modeling career continued to flourish throughout the eighties, as did the insane money that came along with it. I was making ten thousand dollars a day for advertising jobs, and a hundred and fifty thousand when hired for three days to do a spread for a Neiman Marcus catalogue. As supermodel Linda Evangelista famously said once about top-tier models, "We don't wake up for less than ten thousand dollars a day." I know it sounds a bit tacky, but it was true.

As my career continued on the upward swing, I thought more and more about business ventures that could seal my success for years to come. I had had the chance to work with Naomi Sims and watch her develop product lines in the eighties that did fairly well in the marketplace. Very few black women, besides Madame C. J. Walker, the woman who invented the hot iron, had their own line of products, so the idea of following in Naomi and Madame Walker's footsteps appealed to me. Luckily, I would have the chance to meet a woman who could teach me all the essential steps to becoming a success in business: Nikki Haskell.

I met Nikki at a dinner party in New York while I was in the thick of my child-custody case. We became the best of buddies almost in an instant. Originally from Chicago, Nikki was raised in Beverly Hills, studied at the Chicago Art Institute and the New York Institute of Finance, and was one of the first female stockbrokers on Wall Street (she was named stockbroker of the year in 1968). In the 1980s, she was known for hosting some of the hottest parties of the decade, for stars like Michael Jackson and Cher, at Studio 54 and The Underground. She was totally my kind of friend—a strong and fearless woman who wanted nothing more than to see me get higher and higher in my career.

Nikki knew a lot about everything and introduced me to all sorts of people, including the person who signed me to my first major licensing deal. That meeting set me up with a prescription eyeglass deal with Sears department stores nationwide, which was incredibly lucrative and successful for me for many years. Her introductions didn't stop with business, however. She also introduced me to a talented and good-looking actor named Chris Noth. Chris at that time was riding high in his role as Detective Mike Logan on the legal drama *Law & Order*. (He would gain much larger success in the late nineties as the enigmatic Mr. Big on HBO's *Sex and the City*.)

Nikki was fairly certain—aren't they always—that Chris was the perfect new man for me. I didn't care either way, but agreed to accompany her to a dinner where Chris would be. I had dyed my hair a lighter color that night, and I chose to take a vote at dinner about whether or not it looked good. Chris had the most favorable opinion, which I completely dismissed—he barely knew me, so what did his opinion matter? He was OK looking, but nothing to write home about. Later on that night, I walked to the bar to get a drink, and Chris joined me a few minutes later. He came up to me from behind and put his arms around my waist. There was something so calming and reassuring about that gesture that any doubt I'd had about him quickly dissipated. I could see big potential in *Mr. Big*.

But the excitement of meeting Chris couldn't mask what was happening in other parts of my life.

All good things must come to an end, and the opulent lifestyle of the eighties would be no different. The overindulgence and the devil-may-care attitudes of that period had taken their toll and done their share of damage to us all in various ways. AIDS had cut a path directly through the heart of fashion and left pain, heartache, and death in its wake.

The deadly infiltration of drugs and AIDS robbed our industry of the most amazing talent, and me of some incredible friends. Beloved dears like Quintin, Suga, Halston, Willi Smith, and Patrick Kelly all lost their lives. So many were gone in such a short period of time that I was once again overwhelmed with grief. It was becoming too much for me to handle alone in the big city, and I knew it was time for a major change.

Moving to California had been a dream of mine for about a

decade. I yearned for palm trees, for trying out for more film roles. I could take more acting classes, and enjoy the beautiful sunshine twelve months out of the year. I could begin again, and what a joy that would be!

It just felt right to start my life once more at a new address in a new city. I needed a fresh start, and I felt that I deserved a fresh start after all I'd been through.

But that's not exactly how Anansa felt. She was shocked when I told her I was packing up and moving across the country. She couldn't believe I would move so far away from her. She still was fairly satisfied with the arrangement of moving back and forth between her father and me, though in recent times she had realized that her father was taking longer and longer trips away from home to places farther and farther away. Sometimes she had to live for months at time with nannies or sitters while he was away.

As her mother, I hated the fact she had to deal with such a harsh reality at such a young age, but I also knew she couldn't run away from what was real. She had to put on her big-girl pants and make her decision once and for all.

Anansa decided she wanted to come to live with me, but she wanted me to tell Danny. I made it clear to her that she would have to tell her father—she needed to take back control. I wanted her to understand, even at her young age, that she had to be in control of her own destiny, or else risk always being under someone else's thumb.

Ultimately, my daughter did tell her father she wanted to be with me, and he agreed. It was as though it had never been an issue in the first place. He was one crazy man.

~

And so began a new chapter in my life.

Now I had to learn how to parent a preteen full-time. Anansa was accustomed to having her way with her father—this was a child who could write on the walls of the apartment with crayons because Daddy would let her. Getting her to follow my rules, any kind of rules, was going to take some doing, but I had a clear-cut, no-fail plan. I enrolled both of us in therapy—parenting therapy, as well as individual therapy for each of us—and I tried to make it fun. I mixed it up with dance classes, pottery classes, and cooking classes—anything, in fact, that I thought would build more trust and stronger communication between the two of us.

I remember telling Anansa on many occasions to go to her room and scream into her pillow when she was angry with me because that's what the pillow was good for. She would reply, "Oh Mom, what self-help book have you been reading today?"

I had grown up in a time and in a home where your parents weren't your friends, they were your parents, but the situation with Anansa's custody had made a traditional parental relationship more challenging. I wasn't in a position to enforce rules and guidelines the way most mothers would have when she was younger, so I couldn't just pretend we were the regular mother and daughter, because we weren't.

My good friend Nikki, who'd moved back to Los Angeles around the same time I had, was a tremendous help with Anansa. She wasn't a mother, but she had a gang of nieces and nephews and understood Anansa's teenage antics the way that I couldn't—I was too blinded by my love for her and wanting her there with me, after not having her for so long, to really understand.

But with the help of music mogul Quincy Delight Jones—who had just launched Michael Jackson's solo career with *Off the Wall*, *Thriller*, and *Bad*—Anansa was accepted into the very best schools in Beverly Hills, where her classmates were the likes of Nicole Richie, Paris Hilton, and Kim Kardashian. Yes, Anansa was in "high cotton," as the old folk used to say, and Danny had no choice but to foot the bill for her pricey private schooling. I'm sure he loved that!

After Anansa had been in Los Angeles with me a year or so, I encouraged her to read the entire custody court proceedings. I wanted her to fully understand what had happened over the years in court, and what had been said during the hearings by everyone—me, Danny, the judge—everyone. I wanted her to know how her father and aunt had lied. I wanted her to know how hard I had fought for her, and that the case had never been about my being an unfit mother. I needed her to fully appreciate what that custody battle had really been about. I can still remember her curled up in the middle of the floor going through page after page, reading every line. It was imperative that she understood how important she was to me, and what I had endured to make sure I got her back.

Anansa's arrival back in my life full-time again came right on time, and I was ever so thankful. She was a godsend and became my rock as I made the decision to finally face the most drastic change in my life.

I reached out to Alicia's daughter Gigi and asked if I could attend my first AA meeting with her. With my daughter by my side, I was ready to forge ahead into a life without the crutches of drugs, alcohol, and nicotine. From my first meeting at AA, I knew in an instant I was exactly where I needed to be. My recovery wouldn't be a walk in the park, but sitting at those meetings felt like I was on the right track, even though I knew it would be an ongoing struggle. Recovery from any addiction is a continuous process—it's not the end when you kick your habit, only the beginning. Anansa, bless her heart, loved to bring me birthday cakes celebrating the anniversaries of me quitting drinking, smoking, and using cocaine. My daughter was so proud of me, and I was so happy that I could make her proud with every little step. She was still my baby girl, the only person I had anything to prove to.

Ironically, the smoking habit was the toughest of all the vices to quit. I yearned for a cigarette day in and day out, and sometimes the desire was so intense I wanted to crawl out of my own skin. But addiction was something my family had battled quietly for years, and I had to face that reality as well. My father had his issues with alcohol for most of his adult life, and some of his children have walked that same slippery slope with drinking, too.

~

As I eased into my brand-new world of motherhood and normality, I continued seeing a therapist to help me sort out a host of inner demons. But I honestly don't know how I fit motherhood, auditions, modeling assignments, television appearances, and my efforts to stay sober and sane into my daily life. I was fortunate that I had a job that allowed me a certain amount of latitude in my daily dealings. That freedom afforded me the opportunity to attend AA meetings whenever I needed and to focus on any other business I needed to keep my life on track. I was, and I am, blessed.

The blessings continued to flow as Nikki called with news that Chris Noth would be coming out to Los Angeles for a few movie auditions and wanted to give me a call. My mind wandered back to that night at the party in New York and his arms around my waist. I had really appreciated that sense of comfort and security I felt in that moment with him, and I wanted to experience it again. It had been a while since I'd felt that feeling in my life.

My darling daughter answered the phone when Chris called after he arrived—from watching him on *Law & Order*, she'd decided to nickname him Big Nose—and immediately yelled with him in earshot, "Hey, Mom, Big Nose is on the phone."

Teenagers! I can tell you they never warmed up to each other over the course of our relationship. Nevertheless, we had a charming dinner while he was in town, and I could tell that a wonderful new friend/relationship was in the making. The next morning, still on cloud nine, I stepped outside to pick up my *Los Angeles Times* newspaper and noticed my new, very tall neighbor leaving her apartment. She had just moved in across the hall with her boyfriend and young daughter, and I couldn't wait to meet them. I wanted to make as many friends as I could in my new hometown, and I had heard so much about them from the landlord.

As I opened my mouth to say hello, I froze when she turned around. It was Iman!

Why was God playing a trick on me?

I managed a dry smile and a wave as I tried to gather my composure. I had stepped back into the apartment, shaking my head, when Anansa ran up to me with the phone in her hand saying, "Hey, Mommy, guess what?"

I gave her the side eye because I couldn't get over who I had just seen across the hall. My plan was to go back to bed and hope a new day would start.

"What is it, Anansa?"

"Guess who is moving to Los Angeles, not too far from us?" I really didn't want to guess, but Anansa was going to tell me anyway.

"It's Daddy, Mommy! He's moving to Los Angeles in the next few weeks."

All I could think was that God sure has a sense of humor, doesn't he? Taking a page from my mother, I gave my daughter the biggest smile I could muster, and then I picked up the phone and dialed my AA sponsor, Rita, and asked if there was a meeting I could attend.

Rita could tell by my voice that my world was crashing around me, but as she started to pepper me with questions, suddenly, and without warning, I just snapped out of it. My panic subsided, and the shock of what I had just seen and what I had just heard floated away. It hit me that everyone in this life has free will, so Iman could move into whatever building she wanted, and Danny could do what he pleased as well. The only thing l could do was control how I chose to react to their actions, and it couldn't be a repeat of years gone by or I would end up in the same unhappy place. That wasn't going to happen.

So I took a deep breath and finally answered Rita.

"My past was calling, but I refused to pick up. Rita, I'm really looking forward to seeing you at the AA meeting today."

Epilogue

"There is no greater agony than bearing an untold story inside you."

—*Maya Angelou*

For the love of Maya, Ruby, Shirley, Coretta, and all the other "Shero-Angels" who paved the way for my arrival! Thank you!

As I penned this book last year, the world lost two of its most significant cultural powerhouses: the great Maya Angelou and the legendary Ruby Dee. Those two women each single-handedly altered the creative landscape and changed how the world viewed women of color.

I will always treasure the private meetings I had with Ms. Maya over the years. What an amazing honor it was to spend time listening as she offered her words of wisdom to me with such love, sincerity, and clarity, one-on-one. Her books and poems have been such a wonderful refuge for me all my life, and I am so grateful that they now will live on for my daughter and my granddaughter, and for so many other daughters and granddaughters, to appreciate.

Ruby Dee's spellbinding work in film and on Broadway, along with her beloved late husband Ossie Davis, like the writing of Maya Angelou transcends both time and space.

Then there are those phenomenal women who were not creative icons but political dynamos who changed the world bit by bit with the simple power of their unwavering convictions and beliefs. These towering women—such as Barbara Jordan, Shirley Chisholm, Betty Shabazz, and Coretta Scott King—continue to inspire me long after their journey has ended on this earth. These women gave me hope that each one of my dreams was possible—and because of them, it turns out each one was.

Timeline

1952–1969	Born and raised in Buffalo, New York
1969–1970	Attends Northeastern University
1971	Leaves Northeastern and moves to Brooklyn, New York, to start first summer of modeling
1971	Returns to Northeastern University
1971–1972	Moves to New York City with sister Joanne
1972	Moves in with Billy Potter and his parents in Brooklyn, New York
1972	Marries Billy and moves to their first apartment in Brooklyn, New York
1973	Divorces Billy and moves into first apartment in Manhattan
1974	Historic American *Vogue* cover
1975	Historic French *Elle* cover
1976	Marries Danny Sims and moves to 1215 Fifth Avenue
1978	Anansa is born
1979	The film *Ashanti* and album *Don't Lose the Feeling* are released

1981	Files for divorce from Danny and moves in with Johnny Baylor at apartment on Eighty-Ninth Street and Madison Avenue
1982	Loses custody of Anansa
1982	Johnny Baylor dies
1986–1988	Living bi-coastal between New York City and Los Angeles
1988	Moves to Los Angeles to start a new life

Acknowledgments

Tony Abner
Malaika Adero
Richard and Elizabeth Adler
Kim Alexis
Carol Alt
Dr. David Assomaning
Eugene Ball
Peter Beard
Harry Belafonte
Shari Belafonte
Fadil Berisha
Alberteen Bobo
Natasha Iwegbu-Bobo
Francesca Bowyer
Dr. Charles Boyd
Yvonne (Dada) Bratton
 and family
Christie Brinkley
Shaya Byrant and family
Debra and Jerry Carrington
Carol Channing
Nancy Chavez
Nick Chavez
Michael Childers
Jesse Collins

Condé Nast
Eileen Cope
Jeffrey B. Crevoiserat
Judith Curr
Clive Davis
Michael Deflorimonte
Patrick Demarchelier
Talani Diggs and family
Robert Dupont
Robert and Richard Dupont
Kelly Emberg
Terry Fleming
Jane Fonda
Eileen Ford
Leslie Frank
Maggie Fraser
Daisy Fuentes
Helene Galen
Dr. Anath Gerber
Bobby Gerber
Cary Gerkins
David Gernsbacher
Grandchildren Ava, David,
 Dean
Byrant Green

Deborah Gregory
Vijay Gupta
Alan Hamel and Suzanne
    Somers
Dionne Harmon
Rene Harper
Nikki Haskell
Peter Haviland
Bill Hawthorne
Greer Hendricks
Mr. and Mrs. Patrick Herman
    and family
Mellody Hobson
Hollywood and Flame
Lynette and Bob Holmes
Ralph Hughes
Kathy Ireland
Dr. Gail Jackson
Mr. and Mrs. Darren Johnson
    and family
Dustin Johnson and son
My mother, Gloria Johnson
Mr. and Mrs. Leon Johnson and
    family
Sheila Johnson
My father, the late Tim Johnson
Lisa Taylor Jones
Quincy Jones
Elizabeth Kabler
Jamie Kabler
Steve and Cecelia Kamafugi
Bill Kapfer
Lana Kerr

Terry Kim
Gayle King
Harry King
Peter King
Stan Lathan
Drs. Andre and Sonia Lee
Annie Leibovitz
Gideon Lewin
Sandy Linter
Karmisa Little
Sylvia Long
Brian Maillian
Lauren Maillian and children
Ruby Maillian and family
Reginald Mason
Peter Max
Donna MacMillan
Terry McMillan
Ken Meares
Alicia Melkon and family
Bart Michaels
Grace Mirabella
Mr. and Mrs. Henri Mohammed
    and family
Dr. and Mrs. Sanjeev Nath
Ann Marie Neve
Si Newhouse
Bill Nicholson
Tanya Evans Norris and Terry
    Norris
Peter Nygard
Shawn Outler
Anansa Sims Patterson

David Patterson
Leesa Patterson and family
Mr. and Mrs. David Payne
Ron and Jill Perelman
Isabel Perez
Dr. Earl Petrus
Billy Potter
Ralph and Elizabeth Preciado
Gwendolyn Quinn
Joshua Ravetch
Patti Hansen Richards
Ms. Joanne Richardson and
     family
Barbara and Ian Robertson
Allison Samuels
Patty Sicular
Russell Simmons
Karin Silverstein

Barbara Sinatra
Audrey Smaltz
Walter and Karen Sousa
Eileen Stern
André Leon Talley
Cheryl Tiegs
Rita Vale
Rosie Vela
Judy Waddle
Robert Walker
Aaron Walton
Marc Ware
Oprah Winfrey
Mr. and Mrs. Jason Wright and
     family
Mr. Robert Wright and family
Mrs. Sheilah Wright
Mark Zunino

Index